BLOOD ACROSS THE WATER

BLOOD, BRUTALITY AND BETRAYAL: TRUE STORIES FROM THE DARK SIDE OF THE HIGHLANDS

Mark Bridgeman

Watermill Books

Published in 2023 by

Watermill Books
Mill Street
Aberfeldy
Perthshire PH15 2BG
www.aberfeldywatermill.com

British Library Cataloguing-in-Publication Data

A catalogue record for this book is available from the British Library

ISBN 978-0-9957795-5-6

Designed by EMB Graphics, Aberfeldy

Printed and bound in Great Britain by Bell and Bain Ltd, Glasgow.

BLOOD ACROSS
THE WATER

BLOOD, BRUTALITY AND BETRAYAL:
TRUE STORIES FROM
THE DARK SIDE OF THE HIGHLANDS

Mark Bridgeman

Watermill Books

CONTENTS

INTRODUCTION

*My authority may be taken from me
by violence, but I shall never resign it*

Prince Charles Edward Stuart, January 1746

The history of the Highlands speaks to us of a turbulent
and violent past. Despite the remoteness of the landscape,
trouble, it seems, was never far away. This second
collection of short stories follows *Blood Beneath Ben Nevis*
in continuing my examination of the people of Lochaber
through their social history, their quarrels, their thirst
for revenge and justice, and sometimes their sheer
desperation.

During Lochaber's turbulent history, much has been
forcibly taken by the use of violence, as Prince Charles
Stuart and his loyal followers discovered. This collection
of true tales details the harsh reality of life in the

Highlands. Whether in the bustling thoroughfares of Fort
William, the remote Hebridean islands, or the majesty of
Glencoe, the perpetrator of a dark deed seemed to lurk
around every corner.

This compilation of stories adds to those contained in my
earlier book and also seeks to continue them. There is a
continuation of the ongoing hunt for the mysterious lost
Jacobite treasure, and the romance, jeopardy, and drama
of Bonnie Prince Charlie's escape across The Minch to
the islands. In addition to these celebrated stories, made
famous by Scottish folklore, there are tales of ordinary
people committing the most extraordinary acts. Tales of
the cruellest and most desperate murders, and of ghostly
legends testifying to the Highlands' violent past. The
blood spilled on the mainland seems to have seeped
across the water too. The turbulent past of the Hebrides is
also represented here.

Told here for the first time are some newly uncovered
tales, including the story of the body discovered by the
shoreline, the murder on the loch, and the tragic tale
of a husband's cruelty to his wife, which I have called
The Problem With Murder. This dialogue-based chapter is
written in a screenplay style. I hope you find yourself as
drawn into its gloomy universe as I was, while writing and
researching it. In fact, I felt compelled to visit the poor
victim's grave at the beautiful, octagonal parish church in
Dalmally, Argyll. The inscription on the gravestone itself
offers no clue to the tragedy it marks. Nor do the records

of the church reveal the truth. I hope I have managed to do justice to that poignant tale.

Every graveyard, mountainside, cairn, and loch seem to hold yet another ghost from Scotland's brutal past, testifying to this often misquoted passage from the King James version of the Bible:

For all they that take the sword, shall perish with the sword (Matthew 26,26:52)

In Scotland, that certainly seems to be the case.

Mark Bridgeman

www.markbridgemanauthor.co.uk

THE *ANNIE JANE* -
THE STORY OF A TRAGEDY

The protagonist of this story was not a person but a brand new, wooden sailing ship, bound for the shores of the New World. The *Annie Jane* was packed with hopeful emigrants all eager to start a new life in Canada, with all the excitement and trepidation that accompanied that venture.

Tragically, their hopes were dashed on the shores of Vatersay, in the remote Hebridean archipelago of Barra, during a violent storm on Wednesday 28th September 1853. At precisely 11.45pm, in the ethereal pitch black of the darkest night in living memory, with huge breakers crashing around it, the *Annie Jane* ran abruptly aground against the apparent safety of the shallow seabed, close to the shoreline. Within a few minutes one of Britain's worst ever peacetime disasters would take the lives of approximately 350 people, in a largely forgotten story that beggars belief today and still raises more questions than answers. To gauge the enormity of the incident, it is perhaps worth noting that, from an original manifest of approximately 450 passengers and crew, 350 perished on that fateful night – 78% of the total number of souls onboard. A larger proportion even than the 67% of the passengers and crew lost from the *Titanic*, some 60 years later.

What caused such an enormous loss of life that night; and why is the tragedy largely forgotten? Could the shipwreck have been prevented and what happened to the bodies?

Back in 1853, shipwrecks were, sadly, a commonplace occurrence around the shores of Great Britain. The Highland Clearances were also in full swing, as many displaced persons from the Highlands of Scotland, and Ireland too, sought a new life in the Americas, far away from their impoverished existence at home. Scraping together the £3 fare for the passage (close to £400 today), the anxious emigrants boarded the *Annie Jane* at Liverpool Docks in August 1853, with all their worldly possessions in sea chests and carpet bags. The dozen or so more privileged, first class (or cabin class) passengers also boarded. They had paid £10 per head for the voyage and among their number was Captain Charles Rose, who was travelling to Canada to take charge of another vessel, and several members of a French-Canadian Missionary Society, including the Rev J Vernier.

The *Annie Jane* had been recently constructed by Dunning and Baldwin Shipbuilders in the Cape Cove shipyards of Quebec, especially for the Atlantic trade market. Designed to carry both goods and passengers, the *Annie Jane* had sailed for Liverpool to begin her service. After initially failing her safety inspection by Lloyd's of London, she was eventually granted her seaworthiness certification (following some urgent refitting of metal alloy bolts to replace iron and copper bolts that the inspectors had thought likely to rust). The vessel was finally given an A1 rating by Lloyd's, the highest possible safety rating available at that time.

With 45 crew and just a dozen cabin class travellers, the majority of those onboard consisted of 'Steerage Class' passengers, all crammed into the tweendeck, underneath the main deck, and above the lower holds. The tweendeck ran the entire 179 feet length of the ship, yet offered little in the way of natural light or ventilation. Two skylights opened into the main deck above, and a series of narrow, six-inch glass portholes had been placed every seven feet along either side of the tweendeck. The passengers slept in rows of continuous bunkbeds, each approximately 6 feet long and 3 feet wide, and exhibiting an alarming coffin-like appearance (to prevent those asleep from rolling out in stormy seas!). The cramped and stifling conditions were exacerbated by the low ceilings, overcrowding, and the presence of luggage piled up in every corner. Passengers in steerage class were not offered a separate area in which to store their baggage. Small areas were provided for seating, and a galley for the preparation of meals – although there was not enough space to accommodate more than a handful of passengers at any one time. Those in steerage were expected to cook for themselves, although provisions and water for cooking were supplied at a pre-agreed ration. To worsen matters, in the event of the rough seas, all portholes and skylights were closed, and access to the decks was strictly limited, often requiring permission from the captain. The *Merchant Shipping Act*, enacted just the previous year, ensured that the single men were kept in the forward and bow sections, with the married couples and children sleeping midships.

On 23rd August the *Annie Jane* was eventually towed from Liverpool by tug out into the open sea, to commence her maiden passenger voyage. She carried a large and heavy cargo in her holds. As well as various provisions, the ship's holds had been packed with 400 tons of iron, 205 tons of iron railway tracks (bound for use in the construction of the Canadian railroads) and other heavy metal machinery. The *Annie Jane* was estimated to be carrying 1,100 tons of cargo, leaving her with only 10 feet of 'freeboard' – the margin between the main deck and the waterline. For an Atlantic crossing during the stormy autumn season, this offered little safety margin. Partly because of the disaster that was to befall the *Annie Jane* the 'Plimsoll Line' was introduced in 1875, to greater improve this margin and improve ship safety.

Captain William Mason steered a northerly route that took the *Annie Jane* through the North Channel. He intended to sail along the west coast of Scotland before turning west and heading across the Atlantic. However, when northwest of Rathlin they encountered a severe gale. The captain ordered the mainsail and main topsail to be double-reefed. However, as the gale increased in intensity to storm force, the mainsail and jibs were stowed. Passengers were called to man the pumps as the ship began shipping water. The *Annie Jane* seemed to roll and pitch alarmingly, probably from its uneven and over-laden cargo. Freezing torrents of seawater gushed onto the lower decks and the three topmasts snapped sending rigging, sails and spars crashing down onto the deck. With the ship damaged and the rigging torn, a petition was presented to the captain. He reluctantly agreed to turn back and after an uncomfortable voyage down the west coast of Ireland the ship arrived back at Liverpool on 31st August. After repairs, and with most of the passengers back on board (some passengers chose not to return to the ship fearing the seaworthiness of the vessel) the ship left Liverpool again on Thursday 8th September. By this time the actual number of people aboard is unclear. Eyewitness accounts later stated that there were between 400 and 500 people on board the ship as she set sail. In addition, children were not counted on the manifest, meaning that the actual number may have been much higher.

Initially all seemed well, until, at 4pm on Monday 12th September, the ship met another severe gale, which carried away her fore and mizen topmasts, together with the lower mastheads. The crew were then compelled to cut away the jibboom to clear the wreckage. The *Annie Jane* was forced to lay to for almost three days, as the crew rigged a temporary foreyard and set sail once again. However, a second petition was presented by the passengers to the captain; urgently demanding that he 'put back for Liverpool'. Many of those onboard were frightened and imagined the ship to be weakened from its previous skirmish with the seas. To add fuel to the fire, many of the steerage class passengers were furious with their perceived treatment onboard, feeling that they had not been given their agreed allowance of food and water, nor had their complaints been properly addressed during the ship's return to Liverpool.

Night fell and the passengers retired to their quarters, believing that the captain was once again returning to the safety of Liverpool. Their mood lightened noticeably and their tempers subsided. Nevertheless, on waking in the morning, it became evident to the angry passengers that the captain had, in fact, once again set sail for Quebec. They remonstrated furiously with him. Captain Mason, in response, called for his pistol and handcuffs. His crew formed a guard around him. His answer to the passengers, as he menacingly waved his pistol in the air, would later be quoted in all the newspapers and at the subsequent hearing,"Quebec or the bottom! And a bullet for the man who offers to take charge!" The passengers then visibly backed down and retreated. Captain Mason followed them, instructing them to, "Get off my poopdeck, or I will blow your brains out!"

It appears that, as tempers subsided, Captain Mason had a change of heart and agreed to make for the nearest land as soon as the storm abated. However, on the 21st yet another gale pounded the beleaguered *Annie Jane*. She lost her main topsail, mainyard, and the crew had to cut away the main topmast, as the ship rolled alarmingly. The chain cable was dashed from one side of the deck to the other, creating a noise like thunder which echoed and vibrated around the vessel, temporarily drowning out the screams of the female passengers. One of the crew, a Canadian, broke his ankle as it became entangled with the chain. It was nearly impossible to prepare hot food, or to attend to the passengers' needs, as toilets became unusable, vomit filled the tweendeck, and passengers shivered in the dark, terrified, and huddling together for warmth.

The *Annie Jane* continued drifting in the heaving seas, until the evening of the 28th September, with the ship now virtually unmanageable in the full force of the gale.

Finally, the lookout sighted an island.

The unmistakeable sight of breakers dashing against the rocky reefs surrounding the island and the light from Barra Head Lighthouse, told the Captain that Vatersay was in sight. At first a futile attempt was made to avoid a collision by trying to circumnavigate the danger, but Captain Mason quickly realised that his stricken ship, with its uneven and heavy cargo, was being inexorably pushed towards the shore by the gale force winds and the relentless, stormy seas. With four men at the wheel, in the hope of avoiding an even worse collision on the reefs, they attempted to swing the stern as the vessel gradually became sandwiched between the huge waves and the ominously approaching land mass; a large, white sand, crescent shaped bay (visible on his charts as West Bay Beach, or *Bàgh Siar*, on Vatersay). In the growing gloom and in the eye of, what would later be described by witnesses, as a perfect hurricane, the ship, its sails in tatters, tried to avoid the worst of the rocks on the south of the bay as it was forced sideways. First Mate Mr Bell was sent below to warn the terrified steerage passengers of the impending disaster, taking an axe with him in order to knock down the bulkheads dividing the tweendeck. This, he hoped, would give the passengers an unimpeded escape route from the vessel.

At 11.45pm the Annie Jane came to rest silently and softly
against the shallow ground as it neared the shore. She
stopped effortlessly and gently, even though the huge
breakers raced furiously alongside the ship, foaming
around her stern, and the gale force winds buffeted the
stricken ship. None of the passengers had been seriously
injured.

If anyone breathed a sigh of relief, it was short lived. Within
moments the next huge wave smashed into the side of
the ship, lifting it off the bottom and sending it crashing
towards the beach. Captain Mason had positioned two
parties of seamen outside the hatchway doors to prevent
the steerage passengers from coming out onto the deck. As
the ship crashed into the bottom again, however, everyone
was thrown to the side. The foremast was wrenched forward
by the impact, killing the young apprentice who had been
tightly clinging onto the rigging. As the foremast crashed
down onto the deck it smashed through the bulwarks,

making a huge hole in the side of the ship. Freezing sea water gushed into the ship, further weakening the straining hull. Meanwhile, the colossal white breakers picked up the ship, as if it were made of balsa wood, and, turning it broadside, pounded it against the seabed. Screaming in absolute panic, the passengers attempted to rush up the narrow steps of the companionway in an attempt to reach the deck. Many of the weakest were trampled underfoot. Those that did made it up onto the apparent safety of the main deck were half naked, freezing in their night clothes, the men dazed with fear and the women and children screaming in terror. It was completely and utterly dark, making it impossible to even see the person next to you.

Several passengers ran to the front of the cabin and attempted to untie the three smaller boats secured there for emergencies. With the water from the inky black sea surrounding them crashing violently against the rapidly disintegrating wooden ship, the small boats seemed their only hope. However, suddenly and without warning, from the west a tremendous rumble preceded a gigantic wave that smashed irresistibly into the vessel. With one enormous surge, greater than any of the others before it, the huge breaker swept everyone and everything from the deck in front of it. So powerful was the force of the wave that it ripped the galley from the deck like a scoop through butter and smashed the lifeboats to smithereens. In less than 60 seconds, more than 100 passengers were swept into the black void, never to be seen alive again.

When the wave subsided for a moment, just two passengers, from the throng that had gathered on deck, were left.

Charles Smith, a young carpenter, and Julia Macarthy, a mother of twins, remained, clinging onto the mainmast in the blackness. Julia was travelling with her four-month-old twins. Before rushing up onto the deck, she had strapped one of the twins to her back. The other baby she held tightly in her arms. The force of the wave had sheared the four-month-old from her grip and carried it into oblivion.

Meanwhile the violent motion of the breakers broke what remained of the *Annie Jane* apart, like a child's matchstick model, smashing it into three sections, as water continued to pour in upon those still trapped below. With a terrifying crash the mainmast and mizzenmast collapsed, instantly decapitating a young woman who was standing on the poop deck. The ironwork in the ship's hold was lurching violently from side to side, puncturing the hull beneath it. As the ship rapidly filled with water and listed alarmingly, some of the remaining passengers crammed into the poop cabin, screaming for mercy, grateful for the comforting light cast by a few flickering oil lamps.

The French-Canadian missionaries, huddled in the captain's stateroom, prayed for salvation. As they did so another giant and merciless wave smashed into what was left of the ship's hull, finally pulling it apart. The complete middle section of the vessel collapsed under the force of the water and the thousand tons of iron rails in the hold, instantly crushing all those passengers that were still trapped below decks. It was perhaps a merciful ending.

Meanwhile, the survivors, still packed into the poop cabin, screamed as the cabin lurched and dropped deeper into

the water. Now listing at an acute angle, water began to
slowly fill the compartment, extinguishing the oil lamps
and plunging the terrified survivors into absolute blackness.
A darkness which those who have spent all their lives in a
city could not even imagine. Some managed to grab pieces
of floating furniture, some scrambled and escaped through
the skylights. Many others drowned in front of their
comrades, as the paralysing water engulfed them. Those
that managed to escape huddled together on the poop
deck, shivering in the freezing spray, as that section drifted
slowly towards the shore. Many more died of hypothermia
during those long hours.

Miraculously, as dawn finally broke and the sun rose, the
terrified survivors were greeted with a perfect morning.
The sun shone from a calm, cloudless, blue sky onto a
beautiful white beach. By using a fallen mast as a makeshift
bridge, the 60 or so survivors climbed onto the sands to
join the smattering of other survivors who had either
been washed ashore, or who had managed to cling on to a
piece of floating debris. Any joy at seeing these few other
survivors was tempered, however, by the awful sight that lay
before them. From north to south, the beach was littered,
not only with twisted wreckage from the ship, but with the
bodies of hundreds of their dead companions from that
ill-fated voyage. The bodies were disfigured and grotesque.
Naked and bruised, with their limbs and heads crushed,
blood from the victims stained the pristine white sands. So
little warning had been given that most of the passengers
had been either in nightclothes or in a state of undress. As
the survivors turned their eyes towards the sea, the sight of

yet more bodies floating in on the tide greeted them.

Captain Mason gathered the traumatised and shivering survivors on the shore. A swift headcount revealed that 101 passengers had survived, plus one four-month-old baby. As children had not been included in the original manifest, it is impossible to know how many perished on that fateful night.

The behaviour of the islanders and the survivors, from that moment on, seems slightly odd to our modern sensitivities but was extremely understandable at the time. Two large, unmarked mass graves were hastily dug, and the victims' bodies were thrown in 'packed like herrings in a barrel'. No wood was available for coffins and the dead were simply buried as they were found. This may seem insensitive, however there was no legal requirement at that time to register a death (this did not become compulsory under British Law until two years later in 1855), so no definitive list of the casualties was compiled. The extreme trauma exhibited on the bodies of the victims would also have been too much to bear for the already devastated survivors. Unfortunately, the exact place in which the victims were buried has been lost to time, which may account for the tragedy slipping from the public consciousness.

The behaviour of the islanders towards the survivors seems to have been contrasting, depending on whose account is to be believed. Whilst the newspapers that reported the accident in every lurid detail, seemed to praise the inhabitants for the way in which they rallied around the survivors, accounts from the survivors themselves detailed how little support was offered. News of the shipwreck was dispatched to the mainland and rescue organised; however, it seems that those remaining on the island were offered little in the way of food, shelter, warmth or clothing. Although it is highly likely that those eking out an existence on Vatersay and Barra had little in the way of additional food and clothing to offer 100 surprise guests.

It is claimed that local fishermen dragged the remaining bodies to shore and stripped them of their clothes, boots, and any money from their pockets. Rings were also taken from the corpses of the female passengers. Islanders, it seems, were used to cargo and bodies from shipwrecks regularly washing ashore. Sometimes the fruits of such bounty could make the difference between surviving a harsh winter or not.

Captain Mason, in a rather unseemly act, organised a sale of wreckage and remaining cargo from the *Annie Jane*. His swift enterprise infuriated the insurers and owners as, it appears, he had no legal right to do so. He also began the construction of a wooden fence around the burial site, built from timbers salvaged from the wreckage. However, this too was halted by the owners and removed. As a result, to this day, the exact burial site remains a mystery, despite tantalising clues left in the survivors' testimonies. It was "on the shoreline" reported one. "100 yards from the shoreline", testified another. Perhaps we will never know.

An official enquiry was held, in which Captain Mason was largely exonerated, although the efficiency of the crew was questioned, not to mention the dangers of the heavy iron cargo. Whilst many of the survivors discussed the possibility of suing the ship's owners, interest waned, as did the public's interest in the story. There were more than 850 shipwrecks around the shores of Great Britain in 1853, and many more the following year.

Gradually, the remaining wreckage was sold and removed, until the story was almost completely forgotten, had it not been for the unselfish act of a man named Robert Macfie who, whilst sailing in the area several years later, heard the tragic tale of the *Annie Jane* and decided to erect a monument to the events of that awful night. That granite memorial, unseen by many, still sits atop the sandy dunes close to the beach and bears the following inscription:

On 28th Sept. 1853 the ship Annie Jane, with emigrants from Liverpool to Quebec was totally wrecked in this bay and three fourths of the crew and passengers numbering about 350 men women and children were drowned and their bodies interred here. And the sea gave up the dead which were in it. Rev. XX 13

In recent years interest in the story has been reawakened, largely due to a meticulously researched book on the subject, *The Wreck of the Annie Jane*, written by Allan F. Murray. This, in turn, led to a memorial service being held in 2018 to mark the 165th anniversary of the disaster. Perhaps, one day, a suitable memorial will mark the exact spot at which the victims were so hastily laid to rest.

THE CROWN V THE AINSLIE BROTHERS

A most remarkable trial took place at the High Court of
the Justiciary in Edinburgh on Monday 4th December 1854.
Such was the seriousness of the case that the two accused
men were informed that the case would not be heard in
their hometown of Fort William, but before the highest
court in the land. Several officials from Fort William,
including the Sheriff-Substitute, ensured that a significant
amount of pressure was placed upon the authorities to
guarantee that the two brothers from the town would face
a charge of robbery and attempted murder before the most
intimidating bench in the country.

And so, on that Monday morning, dressed in their finest
topcoats and understandably nervous, William and Henry
Ainslie stood side by side in the dock at the High Court
in Edinburgh, as a packed public gallery looked down in
excited anticipation.

William and Henry Ainslie were well respected merchants
who ran a general provisions store in Fort William's
busy High Street. The brothers were long established
shopkeepers, selling a wide variety of household goods,

condiments, and provisions. Both were well respected
and neither had been in trouble with the police before.
However, all that was to change in 1854 when the brothers
employed a shop assistant, a young man named William
Crawford, who had taken lodgings in Kilmallie. From
the beginning of Crawford's employment at the store
the two brothers disapproved of Crawford's odd sense of
humour and general demeanour. He was generally hard-
working and diligent, nevertheless, so the brothers had no
immediate reason to terminate his employment. However,
as the year progressed, William and Henry Ainslie noticed
that several items had mysteriously disappeared from the
store, without a corresponding entry in the shop's ledgers.
Furthermore, several pound notes vanished from their
strong box. One pound, in 1854, was the equivalent of
more than £100 today. William Crawford owned a large
wooden trunk or chest, of which the Ainslie brothers
became suspicious. Crawford often carried it about with

him, an inconvenient and impractical thing to do, and
the brothers became determined to inspect the box.
However, the chest was permanently locked and Crawford
steadfastly refused to grant permission. The final straw
came in the summer of 1854 when the brothers observed
Crawford carrying a highly distinctive and expensive bottle
of raspberry vinegar – identical to several bottles stored at
their High Street premises.

The brothers, completely convinced of Crawford's
complicity in the continuing disappearance of money
from their strong box and of several items from the shop,
applied to the Fort William magistrates for a warrant to
inspect the contents of the mysterious wooden chest.
The process was a long-winded one, partially due to the
bemusement of the officials, who were unused to members
of the public demanding a legal right to inspect another
person's property. Henry and William Ainslie grew
more and more irritated as they impatiently waited for
the warrant. Finally, after several weeks had passed, the
brothers decided to take the law into their own hands.

Two days later, after the shop had been closed for the
evening, the pair followed Crawford back to his lodgings
in Kilmallie. Using the cover of darkness, and hiding in
the shadows, they were able to follow him unobserved. As
Crawford entered the door of his cottage the brothers ran
up to the door and, before the shop assistant could shut
the door behind himself, barged their way inside. Once in
the front room the pair demanded to be given access to the
wooden chest, accusing Crawford of stealing money and
goods from the shop. The young man naturally refuted

the allegation, but this only inflamed the situation further. Voices were raised until Crawford felt so intimidated by the presence of the two men that he reluctantly agreed. Telling the brothers that he needed to find the key to the chest, he went into the back room. William and Henry insisted that he leave the door open, so they could observe his every move (they would later claim that Crawford picked up a cutthroat razor at this point, however this was never proved). The young man returned, claiming he could not locate the key but would try again in the morning. Realising their quest was frustrated, the brothers left, slamming the door furiously as they exited the cottage. With the excitement over for the evening William Crawford retired to bed.

In the early hours of the following morning, Crawford was awoken from his sleep by a loud crashing noise and the splintering of wood. The sudden sound made his heart jump and he hurriedly fumbled for a candle match. However, before he could even light the lamp on his nightstand, the door to his bedroom was thrown open and there, in the dim moonlight from the small window, stood the imposing figures of William and Henry Ainslie. The two brothers seized Crawford, pulled him from his bed and threw him to the floor. Crawford would later claim one of the brothers attempted to strangle him unless he opened the chest. This he did, finally revealing the contents to his employers. Inside were several bottles and boxes of provisions (which the brothers were certain came from their shop); however, each item's label had been carefully removed, thus making it almost impossible to accurately identify their original source or ownership.

Even more mysteriously, there were several packets made
up from single sheets of newspaper, all neatly wrapped
and folded. The sheets of newspaper used to create these
packets all came from recent editions of the *Inverness
Courier*, a newspaper sold locally at that time. Henry
Ainslie carefully unwrapped one of the packets, while his
brother William maintained a vice-like grip on the terrified
young man. Inside each of the packets was a single one-
pound note, neatly folded. The notes were so crisp and
new that the brothers would later describe them in court
as 'silver white as if fresh from the mint'. William Ainslie
strengthened his grip around Crawford's neck while his
brother removed all the pound notes, claiming them for
himself. Crawford protested that the notes were his and
that he had brought them to Fort William with him twelve
months previously.

At this point, events took an even more bizarre twist.
Crawford either fell, or was thrown violently to the floor,
knocking his head. He then seemed to lapse into a state of
semi-consciousness, then quickly into what appeared to be
a coma. The brothers could not revive him, and, in a panic,
Henry ran to fetch the doctor from Fort William.

An hour or so later, Henry Ainslie returned with the doctor,
who immediately examined Crawford. Firstly, as the doctor
would later testify in court, the three men managed to
give the young man a sip of wine, which 'went down quite
slick' and which seemed to revive him slightly. Next the

doctor lit a candle and, by the flickering light of its flame, checked William Crawford's pupils, which appeared to be 'quite natural – which is rather a novelty in a coma'. He then held a bottle of strong ammonia smelling salts under the young man's nose, in an attempt to revive him. However, the patient's reaction was very different from that usually witnessed by the doctor, when reviving someone in this fashion. Crawford jerked his head violently 'from side to side in a deliberate attempt to avoid the titillation', according to the medical man. The doctor also noticed that 'the patient's pulse seemed weak, although his heart was beating steadily and his colour neither came nor went'. Although visibly traumatised, it appeared that William Crawford was out of immediate danger.

With the patient seemingly revived the doctor left and the Ainslie brothers returned to town.

Everything returned to normal for a day or so, although William Crawford did not return to work, until the brothers received a sharp rap on the door and a visit from the Public Prosecutor. Crawford, having recovered from the assault, had wasted no time in contacting the authorities and insisting that his employers were charged. So it was, that on Monday 4th December 1854 William and Henry Ainslie stood in front of the Lord Justice Clerk at the High Court in Edinburgh facing a charge of 'robbery and ferocious assault'. Both men pled 'not guilty'.

In the days before television, cinema and social media, the public gallery at any of the nation's courthouses provided a thoroughly enjoyable, cheap, and warm day's entertainment for the public at large, and the public packed into the High Court expecting a sensational and enthralling trial. Many even brought their own food and drink with them so as not to miss out on any of the 'entertainment'. However, the case of The Crown v William and Henry Ainslie would transpire to be a rather quick and bizarre trial, not at all what those who had packed into the public gallery had anticipated.

The Solicitor-General for Scotland, prosecuting on behalf of the Crown, carefully guided the jury through the events leading to the assault on William Crawford, recounting in meticulous detail the vicious nature of the attack. He highlighted in what manner Crawford had been hurled to the floor, how one of the brothers had attempted to strangle him, and described precisely the vivid bruising around the victim's neck. The doctor's evidence regarding Crawford's weak pulse was also highlighted in indicting just how close the young man had been to his death.

Next came William and Henry Ainslie's defence. In 1854 the accused prisoner at their trial was not permitted to testify for themselves nor have the added credibility of their evidence being heard under oath. It was generally believed by Victorian society that the 'criminal classes' were poorly educated and often dependent on alcohol; meaning they were likely to prejudice their own defence should they be allowed to speak. During any trial it was commonplace to hear a barrister using the infamous defence counsel plea: 'My client's mouth is closed. If he could speak, he might say...'

The privilege which allowed a defendant to testify on his or her own behalf would eventually become more commonplace after an amendment to the law in 1883. However, the right to do so was not fully granted to defendants until the passing of *The Criminal Evidence Act* in 1898. Even then, defendants were still often advised not to testify.

During the Ainslie brothers' trial, their barrister lobbied effectively on their behalf by calling upon the statements and evidence of several men who had seen William Crawford on the morning following the attack. All the witnesses (including Crawford's servant who had arrived early the following morning at the victim's house to serve his breakfast) all testified that Crawford was sitting up in bed laughing and joking. No marks were visible on his neck. Indeed, during the afternoon following the attack, Crawford walked several miles to complete some business he was engaged in. He did not show the least sign of having been injured; and, on the contrary, seemed to be in the highest of spirits. This compelling evidence was further strengthened by the testimony of the doctor who, when cross-examined, stated that Crawford's weak pulse was not unusual and provided no actual proof of any assault. The doctor was also unable to confirm that Crawford had been attacked or thrown to the floor, as had been alleged, but may have merely suffered the effects of an accidental fall.

Following these revelations, and in a piece of pure theatre, a patently angry and infuriated Solicitor-General flung his brief into the air, telling the jury that he no longer wished to proceed with the Crown's case against William and

Henry Ainslie. 'I have not a leg to stand on in the matter of evidence' he declared, and with that, he promptly left the courtroom. A stunned and slightly bewildered Lord Justice-Clerk dismissed the jury and announced to the Ainslie brothers - for the benefit of the rather bemused jury and public gallery:

You may leave the bar without the slightest stain upon your reputation, and that suspicion has not once crossed my mind regarding your guilt.

The verdict was greeted with applause by the vast majority of the audience gathered in the courthouse and the brothers were returned to Fort William as free men.

The trial created a huge amount of speculation and anger within the pages of the Scottish newspapers. Various commentators claimed that the case represented a 'complete breakdown of justice in Scotland', and that the Public Prosecutor had 'trumped up the charges'. Another writer stating that the:

Messrs Ainslie are the victims of a dire conspiracy, at the head of which the Sheriff-Substitute took part! There seems to have been a plot by the officials of Fort William to injure the Messrs Ainslie.

Nevertheless, amid the pantomime style events in the courthouse, two important questions were never answered. Firstly, the question of the brothers' illegal entry into Crawford's house, and their subsequent assault (which was never denied), was never fully investigated. Indeed – as one journalist in the *Caledonian Mercury* pointed out:

The joyful congratulation of these gentlemen by the bench, on them quitting the dock, is altogether misplaced and may be little sympathised by those who had an opportunity of hearing the evidence and seeing the way it was given by the various witnesses.

Finally, the question of the crisp, new pound notes, secreted away by Crawford in his locked chest, does not seem to have been scrutinised. It is perfectly reasonable to assume that William and Henry Ainslie would have noticed so many £1 notes disappearing from their cash box? After all, as mentioned earlier, £1 in 1854 is today's equivalent of well over £100. Therefore, the loss of their money coupled with the suspicious and sudden appearance of several £1 notes in Crawford's wooden chest is, at the very least, an unlikely coincidence. And the unusual fact that the notes were all new and crisp does not appear to have been questioned. Nor why the notes were so carefully folded and individually wrapped.

This raises another tantalising question. Had William Crawford been engaged in robbery, or perhaps even forgery? He certainly seems to have disappeared from Edinburgh, earlier in 1853, at precisely the same time as a spate of forgeries occurred in the capital, only to reappear in Fort William several months later. We do not know why a young man, who was apparently making a comfortable living in the capital city, would suddenly relocate to Lochaber and take an assistant's position in a High Street shop. Having done so, how did he afford to employ the services of a daily servant? This would almost certainly not have been possible on the wages of a shop assistant in a small general store.

Unfortunately, we will probably never know the answers to these questions. William Crawford disappeared from Fort William without a trace shortly after the trial and was never heard of again. The mysterious crisp and new pound notes also seem to have vanished without a trace, although whether they were pocketed by the Ainslie brothers or returned to William Crawford is yet another mystery.

THE BODY
IN THE BRACKEN

Saturday 24th August 1907 had been a beautiful late
summer's day in Scotland, as two men strolled along the
highway, close to the western shores of Loch Linnhe. The
evening had been balmy too. The shadows were long now
as the day drew to a close.

The two friends from Conaglen, a small settlement a few
miles to the southwest, Neil Macdonald, a labourer, and
John Beaton, a crofter, were ambling along the roadway
as they made their way home from Fort William. To their
right the fields swept away, past Stronchreggan House,
leading to the hills behind. On their left, through the thick
bracken, lay 50 yards of marshy grass leading down to the
shoreline where the waters of Loch Linnhe had formed a
small, natural bay. At the point where the road passed the
track to Stronchreggan House on the right, the men were
preoccupied as they chatted in Gaelic, when suddenly John
Beaton noticed a pool of blood on the road. The weather
had been dry and the large amount of blood contrasted
vividly with the lightly coloured, dry and dusty road surface.
Next to the blood were the obvious signs of drag marks, as

if someone or something had been dragged towards the beach on the left. The heel marks of a pair of boots could be clearly seen alongside further bloodstains heading in the direction of the beach. The two men decided to investigate. Broken and flattened branches clearly indicated that the bracken had been bent and pushed to the side, no doubt caused by a large object being dragged through it. Splashes of blood were also visible on the leaves.

Once through the bracken, they could plainly see a flattened trail that appeared to lead right to the water's edge. At first they thought the blood may have been that of a deer shot by poachers. Nevertheless, the impressions of footsteps in the sodden grass puzzled the two men. The trail created by the marks did make an easy path to follow down to the edge of the Loch, however. Close to the shoreline they came across the slumped body of a man on the ground, apparently pushed between two large rocks. The body had been crudely hidden under a pile of bracken and then concealed from view by the surrounding rocks, although it had obviously been secreted in a hurry, as it was easily visible to anyone stood close by. Blood covered the victim's shock of red hair, his face and body, and his clothes were both dirty and bloodstained too. The body was unshaven and poorly dressed in old and worn clothing. His black boots and legs were facing eastwards into the loch, the water gently lapping over them. Blood from a large gash on the man's head had badly disfigured and covered the man's face and tainted the rocks next to his body.

Shocked by the hideous sight, Neil MacDonald and John Beaton hurried back along the road to Fort William to alert the police. Despite the late hour several police constables, an inspector, the procurator-fiscal, and a doctor were immediately despatched to the scene.

An examination of the crime scene, and the resulting post-mortem, produced several clues. There was clear evidence that the body had been dragged from the roadway. From the indications of a scuffle and the large amount of blood present on the road, it appeared that the attack had taken place there. The body had then been hauled 50 yards or so through the bracken and down to the shoreline. It seemed likely to the examining doctor that the man was already unconscious at this stage. The victim had received at least one heavy and savage blow to the back of the head, fracturing his parietal lobe and causing heavy blood loss, followed by two or three smaller blows to the parietal and temporal lobes. There was also evidence of several stab wounds to the torso, probably caused by a small knife with a blade no longer than three inches. Bruising to the body seemed to indicate that the man had also been punched or kicked, probably while slumped on the ground.

Next came the question of the man's identity. He appeared to be about 30 years of age, dirty, unshaven, without a pocket watch or wallet of any kind. However, in the pocket of his jacket was a pedlar's certificate bearing the name Alexander Wilson. At that time beggars and tramps were allowed to earn a living by selling items on the High Street in Fort William, providing they were in possession of a pedlar's certificate granted by the local authority. Without the necessary certificate they would be moved on or even arrested. Pedlars were a common sight in

Fort William and made their living during the day selling
items such as matches, candles, wool, and trinkets; then
they retired to sleep rough in makeshift camps outside
of the town at night. They had earned a reputation for
theft, drunkenness, and for being a general nuisance
to the traders and public in the town. However, it had
been decided that the issuing of licences would curb the
numbers of pedlars and bring only the more respectable
ones into the town.

Criminal enquiries were instigated immediately and
an appeal for witnesses put forward. Crofters and
householders living anywhere along the public road from
the Corran ferry in the south, to Trislaig in the north, were
questioned on the following morning. It soon became
apparent that Alexander Wilson was one of a band of
pedlars who had recently left Fort William and had last
been seen heading in a south westerly direction out of
town. Several witnesses reported seeing the group walking
along the roadway away from Fort William during the
previous day.

Although almost 24 hours had passed, the authorities
believed they might still be able to catch up with the band
of pedlars, whom (it was conjectured by the police) would
have no idea that Alexander Wilson's body had already
been uncovered. Officers commandeered an Argyll
8-horsepower motor car, one of the first cars to grace the
empty roads of the west Highlands, and made a rapid
pursuit along the winding roadway, which soon petered out
into a narrow and bumpy track.

Sometimes their motor car managed to reach speeds of nearly ten miles per hour as it lurched alarmingly along the rutted road surface. They eventually caught up with the group of pedlars on Sunday evening in Morvern,

approximately 20 miles from the scene of the murder. The pedlars were preparing to bed down for the night and had attempted to conceal themselves in the long grass, behind a line of trees, below the narrow track that passes Loch a' Choire, a natural harbour which flows into Loch Linnhe, opposite Shuna Island. The pedlars were startled but offered no resistance. Two men and two women were arrested and taken to the cells in Fort William; Andrew Brown, his wife Katie Stewart, Lindsay MacMillan and his partner Margaret. Brown seemed a surly and bad-tempered character. His furtive behaviour and what appeared to be blood stains on his clothing confirmed the police officers' belief that they had apprehended the right man. Brown, aged 21, was soon charged as follows:

As having on the 23rd or 24th, August nineteen hundred and seven, on or near the public road leading from Corran to Trislaig, in the parish of Ardgour, county of Argyll, did murder Alexander Wilson, a pedlar, of no fixed place of residence, by striking him on the head with a stone or other blunt instrument, stabbing him with a knife or other sharp instrument, and kicking him.

The biggest obstacle faced by the police was corroboration of the story. From bitter experience in such cases, the authorities knew that the group of pedlars were likely to stick together, refusing to co-operate or turn 'King's evidence' on their friend Andrew Brown. Each of the other three were interviewed at length. The officers knew that 25-year-old Katie Stewart, as the accused man's wife, could not be compelled to give evidence against him. However, on questioning her closely, they were surprised to learn that she was not actually married to Andrew Brown; but had merely 'kept company with him for a year and eight months. We lived as man and wife.' She was, in fact married to someone else, but had not seen her real husband for many years. It also transpired that she was related to the deceased man, Alexander Wilson. She was his cousin. A further revelation from Katie Stewart gave the police the motive they wanted to proceed with the case. Katie, although related to the dead man, had previously been involved in an intimate relationship with him. Alexander Wilson had frequently taunted Andrew Brown over this matter, often leading to heated arguments and scuffles, especially when the men had become intoxicated.

Armed with the testimony of Katie Stewart and statements from several witnesses, the murder of Alexander Wilson was deemed serious enough to be tried in the High Court in Glasgow. The case opened on 6th November 1907, Lord Low presiding. Mr William Thomson, acted as Advocate-Depute on behalf of the Crown. He began the case for the prosecution.

The first witnesses called were John Beaton and Neil Macdonald, who described their discovery of Alexander Wilson's body on that Saturday afternoon in August on the western shores of Loch Linnhe. When asked for their opinion they both stated that, from the position of the body, they had formed the opinion that it must have been dragged there.

Next on the stand was Katie Stewart (described in court as 'a female pedlar aged 25'). She would prove to be the Crown's most important witness. When questioned by Mr Thomson, the Advocate-Depute, she answered with the following obviously well-rehearsed and coached speech:

I had been married before, many years ago, but had kept company with Andrew Brown, the accused, for a year and eight months. The deceased Alexander Wilson was my cousin. In August we were in the neighbourhood of Fort William, engaged in hawking, along with a family named Macmillan. On Friday 23rd August, I went to Fort William from Ardgour with Andrew Brown to sell rags and wool. In Fort William we met Alexander Wilson, and we had some drink. On the way back, while crossing on the ferry, Wilson slapped me on the cheek for no reason. When we got to the shore the Macmillans were waiting for us, and we had tea. That would be

*about half-past five. Afterwards we all moved off with our horses,
the Macmillans being in the front. I had occasion to leave Wilson
and Brown for a few minutes, to answer a call of nature.*

*They were making a loud noise with their tongues, arguing, but
they were not striking each other. I did not know what they were
quarrelling about. I looked round and saw Brown with a knife in
his hand. Wilson got a stab on the side of the head. He fell 'canny'
and I saw him get another stab when he was on the ground. I went
on in front and told Lindsay Macmillan and his wife to come back
and separate them. When they came back Brown, who was now
on the beach, chased them back on to the road again. He said he
would 'do the same to her' (pointing to Mrs Macmillan) She went
away. We did not see Alexander Wilson at all. About an hour later
Brown caught up with the three of us, and he now had a cut on
his lip. He said nothing when he came into camp. Next morning
me and Brown went back to see about Wilson; Lindsay Macmillan
refused to go. When we neared the place of the stabbing, Brown left
me at a cairn of stones by the side of the roadway; and was gone
four or five minutes. He said nothing when he returned but 'come
on!' We went straight home again to the camp.*

Cross-examined, Katie Stewart admitted that she had once
been intimate with Alexander Wilson, before she knew the
accused, Andrew Brown. On the day of the tragedy, she also
added that, 'Wilson was trying to pick a quarrel with Brown
and was trying to make him jealous. Wilson was, in the most
filthy way, referring to his previous relations with me.'

Katie Stewart also added that she thought it likely Wilson
had made a sudden attack on Brown first.

Evidence was given by the Macmillans, and a number of
other witnesses who had seen the band of pedlars in the

neighbourhood on that Saturday. Police evidence was also presented, detailing the tracing and arrest of the accused and his companions.

Dr Alexander Cameron Miller, from Fort William, confirmed to the court that he had examined the body:

I thought it was absolutely impossible that the deceased could have fallen, or crawled into the position where he was found. The external marks of injury consisted of twenty-two wounds, eighteen of them being on the head, face, and neck. There was one main fracture, encircling practically the whole of the skull, with two subsidiary fractures. I am of the opinion that death was caused by violent blows applied by means of some heavy article or implement, wielded with great force and causing extensive fractures of the bones of the skull. I am also inclined to the view that the deceased was still alive, though unconscious, when placed in the hollow where the body was found.

A Gaelic speaking crofter was called to the stand, and his evidence was translated for the benefit of the jury. He reported bumping into the accused about twenty-five yards from the spot where the body was found. From the accused man's appearance, the witness thought, 'there was definitely something wrong. Round about his mouth there was blood, which seemed to be fresh.'

Although changes to the law in 1883 and 1898 meant that defendants could now speak in their own defence (as discussed in the preceding chapter and in my previous book *Blood Beneath Ben Nevis*), they were still frequently advised not to do so, as it was felt likely they would incriminate themselves or prejudice their own defence. In the case of Andrew Brown, described by the newspapers as 'of the lower or tinker class', it was felt that his best chance of an acquittal lay in a pre-prepared declaration being read out on his behalf during the trial. Brown's rough manner and surly appearance were thought likely by the defence to colour the jury's opinion of him.

DECLARATION OF ANDREW BROWN
(twenty-one years of age and a hawker,
having no fixed place of residence)

Kate Stewart travelled with me as my wife, though we were not married. On the day of the tragedy we had met Alexander Wilson; and were in Fort William with him for some time and had some drink. We all crossed on the ferry to Trislaig and started for our camp. Wilson, on Kate's invitation, joined us. At a wooden bridge on the road we met a tall, dark-whiskered man of the tramp class, who seemed to know Wilson. At Wilson's request I gave the tramp some drink. Latterly Wilson turned back with the stranger, asking us to return and meet him at the same place next morning. Meanwhile Kate had gone on ahead with my horse and did not see us encounter the dark whiskered stranger. Following the departure of Wilson with the stranger I walked after my wife and arrived at the camp soon after her. We both retraced our steps in the morning to meet Wilson, according to my promise, but did not see him. I declare that I know nothing of how Alexander Wilson came by his death. Several times before we had parted on the previous day Wilson was impudent to me, but I paid no attention.

For the defence, two passengers who had crossed on the
ferry with the accused, testified that Alexander Wilson was
'very drunk and quarrelsome, so much so that the ferryman
took out the tiller rod and said he would hit him with it If
he did not keep quiet.'

The Rev JB Crawford, the Parish Minister of Kilmallie, also
testified that he had been at Trislaig Schoolhouse on the
evening of 23rd August, where he had witnessed a band of
tinkers of whom the accused was one. He also confirmed
that a red-haired man had climbed off the ferryboat with
Andrew Brown and Kate Stewart. According to the minister
the red-haired man (who matched the description of the
deceased), 'used extremely coarse language with regard
to previous acquaintance with the woman. His manner
was exceeding provocative, and the accused behaved with
patience that was amazing.'

With that the defence rested their case and Lord Low
instructed the all-male jury to retire and consider their
verdict. Andrew Brown was returned to his cell to nervously
await his fate.

After an absence of just five minutes, the jury returned a
unanimous verdict of culpable homicide against Andrew
Brown. Lord Low told them that he:

entirely agreed with their verdict in this case. I quite recognise the
great provocation under which Brown acted; and am even ready
to believe that Brown was not the offender in the first instance.
Yet the retaliation which Brown made was so extravagantly out
of proportion to any sore from which he had suffered, and to show
such a degree of violence was extraordinary. I do not think I have

come across a case in which so many serious injuries were inflicted.

Ultimately Brown's claim of a 'dark whiskered stranger' who conveniently appeared, but was not witnessed by anyone else, was improbable and not likely to be believed by a jury of respectable middle class Edwardians, who were naturally prejudiced against the 'tinker class' at that time.

However, despite his stern words, Lord Low passed the comparatively lenient sentence of just seven years' imprisonment on Andrew Brown for such a brutal killing. Perhaps a reflection of his understanding of the extreme provocation Brown endured, the drudgery of the tinkers daily life, and the loathsomeness of Alexander Wilson's character.

MURDERED FOR ONE POUND

The year 1856 was gruelling enough for the poorer working classes across the mainland of western Scotland. It was even more so on the Inner and Outer Hebridean Islands.

A succession of poor harvests and even worse weather had left large swathes of the population hungry and destitute. *Gaiseadh a' bhuntàta*, the Highland potato famine, had blighted the agricultural communities of the Hebrides and the western Highlands for almost a decade. The potato crop (upon which the rural population had become over-reliant) had been repeatedly hit by potato blight, a fungus-like micro-organism that devastated the harvest and as a consequence, destroyed the livelihood of thousands. As always seems to be the case, the poorest were hit the hardest. On the island of Barra, for example, the population were described by the island's parochial board as being in 'poverty beyond description, the most destitute peoples we have ever seen'.

Despite major charitable efforts by the rest of the United Kingdom to alleviate starvation, the terms on which charitable relief was given led to impoverishment and

malnutrition amongst its recipients. In an archetypal
example of topsy-turvy Victorian philanthropy, charitable
relief was offered by paying minimal wages in return
for hard labour on public work schemes. This kind of
'relief' was not even made available to those with any type
of disposable capital (which was interpreted to include
livestock). A daily ration of oatmeal was given by the
Central Relief Board - 24 ounces per man (later reduced
to 16 ounces), 12 oz per woman and 8 oz per child. This
equated to one small bowl of porridge a day for a working
man. Recipients were expected to work for their rations on
public work projects, such as the building of 'destitution
roads'. Often these schemes were of little real value to the
community. With the island of Barra in bankruptcy, tenants'
livestock was sold to pay rent arrears. The frugal new owner
of Barra, John Gordon of Cluny, also did little to help the
residents. He eventually died in 1858 and was described as
'the richest commoner in Scotland', leaving behind more
than £2 million (the equivalent of more than £250 million
today).

With emigration to Australia, Canada, or the mainland,
seemingly the only option, it is estimated that a third of the
population of the western Scottish Highlands emigrated
between 1841 and 1861. The final straw came for one
resident of Barra, William Guthrie, in 1854. Rather than
be dragooned onto one of John Gordon's emigration ships
to Canada, or accept the lower daily oatmeal ration, he
instead chose to move to the mainland in search of work
and lodgings.

William Guthrie found a room to rent in an isolated
Lochaber farmhouse, close to Loch Linnhe, and
immediately found employment as a mason and labourer.
The work was hard, and Guthrie was no longer in the flush
of youth, already more than 60 years of age. He was often
required to undertake a long and arduous journey to work
on foot.

In 1855 he was hired by a contractor, the work requiring
him to walk many miles south every week, through lonely
and isolated forests and glens, often returning late at night.
It was, nevertheless, regular pay and more money than he
had ever seen while struggling on the island of Barra. On
a bitterly cold New Year's Eve in 1855, William Guthrie
finished work, with the gratifying knowledge that he was
not required to attend the following morning. He had also
just collected a fortnight's wages, amounting to £2 3s 4d
(approximately £220 today), and his mood had lightened
considerably. Calling into the home of Mrs Barnes, whose
parlour also doubled as a public house serving whisky to
passing workmen and navvies, he fortified himself with a
'nip' for the long and cold return trek to his lodging. The
mood in the inn was jovial, with several other workmen also
enjoying a dram and Mrs Barnes only too keen to ply them
with spirits in an effort to help reduce the weight of their
pay packets.

A young 26-year-old man named Robert Gordon sat quietly
at one of the tables. He lodged with Mrs Barnes and often
sat among the labourers as they drank, engaging them
in spirited conversation, hoping to be the beneficiary

of their generosity, as he was invariably short of money. Guthrie bought Robert Gordon a drink and the two men chatted agreeably about the bitterly cold weather and life in general, until Guthrie excused himself, telling Gordon that he needed to buy more tobacco from Mrs McFarlane's grocery shop in the village before returning to his lodgings. Gordon smiled and nodded, telling Guthrie that he would walk with him as he, too, needed to buy some tobacco.

The two men left the inn together. Once in the grocery shop, Robert Gordon observed Guthrie remove a tobacco tin from his inside waistcoat pocket. As Guthrie paid for his provisions, Gordon noticed two £1 notes inside the tin. After paying, Guthrie replaced the tobacco tin in the inside pocket of his waistcoat. Hurriedly, Robert Gordon excused himself from Guthrie's company and left the shop. A short moment later, Guthrie left too, buttoning his jacket against the biting cold. William Guthrie glanced in both directions. Despite Robert Gordon having only left the shop premises only a few seconds earlier, the roadway appeared deserted. Guthrie had hoped for company on his return trek to his lodgings, but quickly resigned himself to the long walk alone. He set off along the roadway, with the only light coming from the waxing crescent moon and the stars reflected in the shimmering loch. After travelling a mile or so, passing the occasional horse and cart, he turned along the long and windy track that led to his farmhouse lodgings, burdened with a slight sense of apprehension, from a sixth sense that someone had been lurking in the shadows a few hundred yards behind him during his lonely journey.

The following morning, New Year's Day 1856, at around 10 o'clock, Mr and Mrs William Smith, the owners of the farmhouse in which William Guthrie lodged, were surprised not to find him in his bed. They both assumed that he been celebrating Hogmanay rather too enthusiastically and would return later in the day, no doubt, the worse for wear.

As they nodded disapprovingly to each other, Mrs Smith noticed Guthrie staggering along the track towards the house. She turned to her husband and motioned towards him. Guthrie, they observed, appeared to be very much intoxicated. His hat was missing, he seemed to be lurching uncontrollably, his clothing was muddy and stained, and his face was scratched, as if he had fallen many times on his journey home.

At first, Mr and Mrs Smith expressed their disapproval, as Guthrie staggered towards them. They had thought him to be of fairly temperate habits and would certainly have not rented a room to him, had they known him to be a heavy drinker. However, as he drew nearer it became clear he was not intoxicated but deathly pale. Guthrie collapsed in front of his landlords, and gasped, 'I have been nearly murdered, they have taken all that I have!'

The Smiths put Guthrie to bed, settled him as best they could and told him to rest.

The following day Guthrie's condition appeared to have worsened and Mr Smith proposed sending for the doctor. However, it was decided to contact the local police officer, Constable Young, as it was feared Guthrie would not survive another night.

Constable Young was summoned and, on arrival, was met with the sickening sight of a man almost certainly in the last throes of life. The police constable immediately took out his notebook and pencil from his tunic pocket and wrote down Guthrie's deposition, as the poor man struggled to form his words as he winced in pain, clutching his side:

I was returning home along the road on Monday night, between 10 and 11 o'clock, when I heard some persons coming up behind me. I was suddenly assailed by three or four navvies, who seized me so desperately by the throat that the blood sprang from my mouth, my nose, and my eyes. They then threw me down, robbed me of all I had, and jumped upon my belly till I became insensible. Robert Gordon was one of these men; the others I did not know. On coming to, I crawled to the shelter of some oat-stalks, on the roadside, and lay there all night, and on the following morning made my way, with great difficulty, to the farmhouse.

These would prove to be his final words. Shortly afterwards
William Guthrie slipped into unconsciousness before
passing away the following morning.

Robert Gordon was arrested at his lodgings a few days after
Guthrie's dying statement had been taken, and he was
charged as follows:

*Robert Gordon, you are charged with murder and robbery, in so
far as, on the 31st December or 1st January last, not far from the
Lochaber farmhouse, occupied by William Smith, you did beat and
assault William Guthrie, mason, and did seize him by the throat
and knock him down, and kick and strike him in the side of the
belly, and did otherwise maltreat and abuse him, by which the said
William Guthrie was mortally wounded in his person, and his
liver was ruptured, in consequence of which he died on the 3rd day
of January, 1856; and that you took by force and violence, from
Guthrie a £1 bank-note, 21 shillings, or thereabouts, in silver, and
several articles, including a quantity of tools.*

A trial date was set for Tuesday 6th May 1856 at the Spring
Circuit Court of Justiciary in Glasgow, with Lord Cowan
presiding. Gordon pled 'not guilty'.

The trial was to prove a remarkably interesting one for
several reasons, especially when the case seemed, on paper
at least, to be a straightforward one.

Firstly, the post-mortem evidence verified that William
Guthrie had suffered three fatal ruptures to his kidney,
which the examining doctor, Dr Robert Buchanan,
confirmed were the cause of death. The defence attorney
argued that these injuries could have been caused by a

bad fall; however, Dr Buchanan stated to the court that the ruptures were 'far more likely to have arisen from a series of kicks and blows.'

The prosecution then turned their attention to the behaviour and actions of Robert Gordon in the hours following Guthrie's death. A steady stream of witnesses was presented to the court. Firstly, it was confirmed that Gordon and Guthrie had left Mrs Barnes' public house together. Secondly, Margaret McFarlane remembered Robert Gordon coming into her grocery shop with William Guthrie. She confirmed that, while Guthrie was paying for his goods, 'the prisoner was standing by him, and saw that he had money.' She was also able to confirm that, 'during the following day, the prisoner bought two shillings and sixpence worth of spirits, despite usually not having any money to speak of.'

A labourer named James Glen testified to witnessing Robert Gordon with a tobacco tin containing five shillings, and to seeing him on New Year's Day, drinking heavily in a public house with 'handfuls of money'.

Several witnesses also testified to remembering seeing some spots of blood on Gordon's smock and to observing him attempting to wash it the following day. The defence argued that 'the tiny amount of blood could not have resulted from an attack on William Guthrie, which surely would have created a great deal more.' The defence also claimed that Gordon had appeared calm and unflustered the following day, not changing his behaviour in any way, nor attempting to conceal his bloodstained smock.

Next, James Hunter, a labourer who had been working alongside Robert Gordon, told the court of a drunken argument that had taken place between himself and the prisoner on the evening following the murder. Robert Gordon, Hunter informed the jury, had broken the door into his home that night. When the two men had argued about the cost of replacing the door, Gordon had replied, 'I have plenty of money for that now.'

The forensic examination of the crime scene was remarkably sophisticated considering the era and the low profile, rural nature of the crime. In 1856 there was little in the way of forensic evidence used in court cases. Neither had the process yet been made fashionable, as it would become two decades later, thanks to the Sherlock Holmes' stories by Sir Arthur Conan Doyle. Although Scottish chemist James Marsh had pioneered the use of scientific testing in a court case 20 years earlier, the use of photographic evidence, fingerprinting and blood groupings was still half a century away.

Meanwhile, a thorough combing of the crime scene by two local police constables had uncovered a patch of trampled ground, where it appeared that the assault had been committed. In addition, a number of articles belonging to Guthrie were found lying in the grass, including his tobacco tin and the lining from the inside pocket of his waistcoat, which had been torn out during the robbery. Several pieces of broken tobacco pipe were also found discarded close by and were presumed to belong to the three men. These items were carefully collected and presented in court.

It seemed an open-and-shut case to the prosecution; however, the defence had a clearly defined strategy. They intended to create doubt in Gordon's guilt, by creating a degree of uncertainty in the jury's mind, ultimately meaning they would be forced to find the defendant not guilty. Robert Gordon's solicitor skilfully implied that one of the other two men had actually inflicted the lethal blows upon Guthrie's body, leaving Robert Gordon as merely an unwilling bystander.

Finally, a statement from Robert Gordon was read aloud by the Clerk of the Court - prisoners in 1856 were not permitted to speak in their own defence during a trial, as it was generally thought that the 'criminal classes' were highly likely to prejudice their own case, due to their lack of intelligence and generally poor level of education.

Gordon's declaration to the court claimed that he was present while the two others, Hugh McKay and John Wilson, had attacked Guthrie, robbing and assaulting him. Robert Gordon stated that:

it was Wilson who wanted money, and attacked Guthrie on the road, seized him by the throat, threw him down, kicked him, and took his money. I received six shillings of it on the spot, and some silver the next day. I was also afraid of Wilson splitting upon me and blaming me.

That concluded the evidence for the defence and, following the judge's summation, the jury retired to consider their verdict.

After an absence of 60 minutes, the jury returned. They were not swayed by the defence's persuasive arguments. Robert Gordon was found guilty of murder. However, the jury did unanimously recommend that the judge show leniency in his sentencing, due to the prisoner's youth and their belief that, at the time the robbery was committed, murder was not premeditated. Nevertheless, Lord Cowan was unmoved. He donned his black cap and sentenced Robert Gordon, 'to be to be hanged at Dumbarton on Thursday, the 22nd instant.'

Gordon, who had remained calm and unmoved during the trial, broke down and had to be assisted to his cell.

Despite the heinous nature of the crime, there appears to have been much public disquiet at the harsh sentence. A petition was raised and delivered to Buckingham Palace, in which it was claimed that a mere accessory in a crime should not be sentenced to death. Queen Victoria, it appears, agreed, writing a letter to the Sheriff Substitute of Argyllshire requesting that the idea of a reprieve be entertained in the case of Robert Gordon.

Sure enough, the wheels of justice eventually turned. Robert Gordon's sentence was commuted to transportation to Australia for life, dooming him to become one of the 162,000 men transported to the colonies between 1787 and 1868. On 18th September 1857 Gordon was placed in iron shackles aboard the *SS Nile* and, along with 270 other convicts, set sail for western Australia.

As for the two other men involved in the brutal attack on William Guthrie. there was little evidence obtained during the investigation with which to charge them. William Guthrie had been unable to identify them in his deathbed statement; and the accusations made by Robert Gordon regarding their involvement was regarded as little more than hearsay.

John Wilson was arrested and held in custody for three weeks, although he was eventually released without charge. Hugh McKay was questioned at length about the incident. However, he was able to persuade those questioning him that he was not involved in the assault - perhaps the revelation that he was a former police constable being enough to convince the authorities of his innocence!

Robert Gordon would never return to his native Scotland. After a gruelling ocean crossing, the *SS Nile* eventually reached land in western Australia on 1st January 1858 – 105 days after departing Scotland and, in a macabre coincidence, on the second anniversary of the murder of William Guthrie.

On arrival, Gordon was incarcerated in Fremantle Prison, Perth and, as part of his sentence, was expected to perform up to ten hours a day of hard labour, often in searing heat. Any failure to do so could be punished by flogging, solitary confinement, the treadmill, or the enforced wearing of heavy leg-irons.

After enduring eight years under this punitive system, Gordon was granted a conditional pardon on 1st October 1866 (called a Certificate of Freedom). Convicts were then allowed to return to Britain – but only at their own expense. Since fares were so high, this made the chance of seeing their homes again an impossibility for the majority of ex-convicts.

Robert Gordon was forced to remain in Australia and, weakened after years of hard labour and the harsh environment, died on 11 December 1868 at the age of just 39.

MOUNTAIN MYSTERIES
(PART ONE)

Towering above Loch Linnhe, at the western end of the Grampian Mountains, sits the highest mountain in Great Britain, the enigmatic Ben Nevis. Extensively shaped by glaciation, this volcanic rock superstructure reaches an elevation of 4,406 feet (1,343 metres). At the summit lies a plateau of about 100 acres, sloping slightly to the south, and with a sheer face to the northeast. Snow can lie on certain parts of Ben Nevis throughout the year, and permafrost conditions are almost reached. With its summit often shrouded in an ominous mist, the mountain seems to hold many secrets which it seems strangely unwilling to surrender.

The first mystery, it appears, seems to have been the confusion over the title 'Britain's highest mountain'. Initially Ben Nevis was not considered to be Scotland's (or Britain's) highest peak by many geologists. That honour was thought to belong to Ben Macdui in the Cairngorms National Park.

The first recorded ascent of Ben Nevis was made five years before the American War of Independence, on 17th August

1771 by James Robertson, an Edinburgh botanist, who was travelling in the western Highlands collecting botanical specimens (or possibly searching for valuable minerals from which to make his fortune). Despite Robertson recording that 'the summit far overtops the surrounding hills' many still believed that Ben Macdui was the higher peak. The second known ascent took place in 1774, when John Williams surveyed Ben Nevis's geological structure and decided there were no valuable minerals to be found. Many more were to attempt the climb, including the poet John Keats, who climbed the peak in 1818, and likened the experience to 'mounting ten St Paul's Cathedrals without the convenience of a staircase.'

What is less well known is the slight feeling of disappointment experienced by James Robertson and John Williams, who both found debris and artefacts on the summit, strongly suggesting that others had been there many years earlier.

However, interest in Ben Nevis had been aroused. The first Ordnance Survey team to map and measure Ben Nevis in 1847 was able to confirm its height as 4,409 feet (1,344 metres), rising a full 111 feet (35 metres) above Ben Macdui. Now officially the highest mountain in the land, Ben Nevis would draw visitors from all around the world. Over the coming years, as climbing and equipment slowly became more sophisticated, Ben Nevis would gradually give up the answers to several mysteries. Nevertheless, many other mysteries have still to yield an answer.

Heavy snow fell early in October 1899, with large amounts

covering Ben Nevis from just a few hundred feet above sea level. Temperatures plummeted to six degrees below zero at the peak. Those working at the recently opened observatory on the summit communicated with the town below, on the newly installed telephone, to report a strange and otherworldly howling which echoed around the snow topped mountaintop. The men were effectively trapped, and the eerie baying terrified them. In blizzard like conditions, with near zero visibility, the astronomers wondered what could be causing the ghostly wailing sound. They knew of no climbers on the mountain on such a snowy and dark night. As the sound seemed to get nearer and nearer to the building, echoing above the roaring wind and blizzard, one of the men, Angus Rankin, grabbed a lantern and bravely opened the door into the cold and pitch-black night. The white carpeting of snow reflected the light from his lantern. All around him was a flurry of snow framed against the jet-black sky. Suddenly, Rankin sensed a movement on his right side. Turning quickly, he looked down to see a black, white and tan Border Collie dog sat by his side. The dog was shivering and scared, its matted fur covered with snow and ice. After the initial shock, the dog was invited inside the observatory to warm up.

When the men were able to return to the town a couple of days later, they made a concerted effort to find the dog's owner. No one, as far as they could determine, had been on the mountain that night. There were no visitors or climbers known to be on Ben Nevis. If the dog had belonged to a climber, who had unfortunately perished in the cold, nobody was ever found. Neither had the dog been reported missing. Exactly what had persuaded the collie to climb more than 4,000 feet above sea level in such a snowstorm was never discovered (although measurements taken at the observatory do sometimes record a higher temperature at the summit than at the base!). The dog was never reclaimed, despite the story being reported in several newspapers, and a home was eventually found for him. Happily, the collie was not harmed by his adventure and lived for many more years, frequently enjoying a return trip to the mountain with his new owner.

The observatory, which undoubtedly saved the dog's life, closed in 1904. It is also interesting to speculate if the author Sir Arthur Conan Doyle, himself a Scot and a believer in all things supernatural, was inspired by the story of a ghostly dog howling in the wilderness while researching his novel *The Hound of the Baskervilles*, which was first published two years later.

The mystery of the dog found at the summit of Ben Nevis did not end there, however. Just three years later, Robert MacDougall, one of the astronomers at the Observatory, heard an unusual squeaking sound emanating from the visitors' room. On investigation he discovered a pure white fox terrier with a litter of six pups in a box hidden the corner. The presence of the animals was a complete mystery to staff at the observatory. Was there really a family of feral dogs living and surviving in the harsh conditions atop the mountain, or had someone carried the puppies 4,000 feet to the summit, just to abandon them? The mystery was never solved, although happily homes were found for all the animals.

An enigma of a more religious nature occurred in April 1905 when the Rev M Robertson, a prominent member of the Scottish Mountaineering Club, suffered an horrendous experience while descending Ben Nevis. Despite being advised that the weather was unsuitable for climbing, there having been an almost continuous fall of snow that day, accompanied by thunder and lightning, Rev Robertson set out alone to make the ascent. He reached the summit safely before starting his return journey. Holding on with his ice axe, he had just begun to descend a steep and dangerous snow slope, when a huge and vivid flash of lightning struck his metal axe jolting him and sending him plummeting over the slope. Rev Robertson cascaded approximately 1,000 feet downhill until his progress was halted was some thick bushes. He lay unconscious in the freezing cold for several hours, before coming to, and dragging himself in a dazed and confused state to his hotel in Fort William. He recollected nothing from the moment the lightning struck his axe. Despite his several injuries, including large gaping wounds, and a multitude of bruises, he made a full recovery. How he escaped death was a complete mystery, especially to those who were familiar with the particularly treacherous spot in which the accident had occurred. It was assumed by many that a higher power had been protecting the lucky clergyman on that particular day!

Just as mysteriously, in June of the same year, a Royal Marine stationed aboard *HMS Highflyer* on Loch Linnhe, decided to attempt an ascent of Ben Nevis single-handedly. He experienced a similar fall to the Rev Robertson and suffered a fractured skull and other horrendous injuries. Yet he somehow managed to make his way down, in complete darkness and unaided, eventually being discovered unconscious on Fort William Public Pier several hours later. He too made a miraculous recovery.

Not surprisingly, given the number of lives lost on the slopes of Ben Nevis, visitors claim to have seen not one, but two, ghosts haunting the mountainside. Conceivably in response to the myth of 'The Grey Man of Ben Macdui', or perhaps caused by the unnerving shadows that tend to be reflected from lanterns onto the snowy escarpments, the two apparitions are affectionately known as 'Penny Plain' and 'Twopence Coloured.' The latter is a distinguished ghost. Reputedly the brother of the famous Brocken Spectre from Germany, 'Twopence Coloured' has only appeared on rare occasions, usually on sunny days. The ghost can be seen as a shadowy form on the northern face of the mountain.

'Penny Plain' was viewed more frequently by Victorian and Edwardian climbers, 'raised at night with the aid of a bull's-eye lantern', with his head 'surrounded by a white glory.'

On Saturday 1st November 1925 the unmistakable
sound of a gunshot echoed around Ben Nevis. It was
a clear and calm day as the sound reverberated across
the mountainside. The only people known to be on the
mountain that day were a team of 'gangers' employed
by Balfour, Beatty & Co on the Lochaber Hydro Electric
Scheme. The Fort William police were called, and they
immediately contacted the company. A swift headcount was
made of all the men known to be at the site. One name was
missing from the list of men present - John A MacLeod. He
had last been seen on the preceding day carrying a rifle,
leaving the hut where he resided. MacLeod had informed
the hutkeeper that he intended to climb the slopes of Ben
Nevis in the hope of shooting a stag. When he had not
returned the following morning, the hutkeeper become
anxious and informed the authorities. The police were
certain that the two incidents were linked, and a search
party was quickly organised. John MacLeod was extremely
popular, and twenty men immediately volunteered to assist.

As a result, the slopes of Ben Nevis were comprehensively
scoured for many hours. The search was about to be called
off for the day, as dusk fell, when one of the party made
a tragic discovery. John MacLeod's body lay among the
heather on the side of the mountain, at an altitude of about
1,500 feet. The greater part of his head had been blown
clean off by the force of the gunshot. Rapid rigor mortis
had left MacLeod's corpse in a haunting and shocking
position, which visibly shook the team that discovered
him. The dead man's hands still clasped the rifle, with the
muzzle pointing to the face, his left hand still gripping the

barrel and the forefinger of the right hand on the trigger.
John MacLeod was an extremely heavy man, and it was
deemed inadvisable to remove the corpse in the darkness
from such a height. Consequently, John MacLeod's body
was covered up for the night to guard against depredation
by foxes and ravens. The following morning a sombre
group of MacLeod's colleagues ascended to the spot; and
brought his body back to the base camp for burial. No one
could think of any reason why MacLeod would have taken
his own life, or why he had chosen the lonely mountainside
to perform the terrible act. Ben Nevis had claimed one
more victim.

In April 1939 two mysterious and rather well-spoken
young English men in a motor car called at the Belford
Hospital in Fort William, asking if they could borrow the
hospital's only Alpine stretcher, stating that a mountaineer
had fallen from a cliff on Ben Nevis and was lying on the
mountainside with a broken leg. They were provided
with the stretcher and the two men were observed by
hospital staff as they appeared to be heading towards the
mountaineers' hut, which lies at the foot of the north-
eastern buttress of Ben Nevis, approximately 2,000 ft.
above sea level. Nothing was heard from the young men
for some considerable time, however, and, concerned for
their welfare, a search party was quickly organised from
Fort William. Just as the search teams were receiving their
instructions, a party of climbers from the Cambridge
University Camping Club were seen leaving the town, in
high spirits, drinking and singing as they sped away. From
the windows of their car the hospital's alpine stretcher

could be clearly seen, strapped to the car's roof! A youthful student prank, no doubt, but alas it was the hospital's only specialised alpine stretcher. Despite a plea to the authorities at the university, the stretcher was never returned.

Just four months later, in August 1939, with all eyes turned apprehensively towards Europe as war with Germany seemed inevitable, preparations for the defence of the country were in full swing. Gas masks had been issued, blackout instructions circulated, and wartime regulations prepared. The population looked suspiciously over their shoulders for signs of German spies and 'Fifth Column' activity. From her kitchen window in Lochy Bridge Cottages, Mrs Ross described a huge 'wall of water, 100 feet high and 20 feet wide rising like a huge fountain' on the Carn Dearg ridge, behind the Ben Nevis Distillery, at the foot of Ben Nevis. The huge jet of water appeared at 11 o'clock in the morning, gushed high in the air for a few minutes, showering water down like a thunderstorm, before receding, only to reappear at regular ten-minute intervals until 2 o'clock in the afternoon. Mrs Ross reported the matter to the police, 'I was startled as the ground rumbled and vibrated. Firstly, I thought Ben Nevis had become volcanic. Then I thought the Nazis had sabotaged the water pipeline'.

Engineers from the British Aluminium Company were despatched to the area and climbed up to the ridge gate. Adjacent to the ridge lay the five pipes which conveyed the waters of Loch Treig through the Ben Nevis tunnel to the aluminium company's power house at Fort William. The phenomenon, it was believed had been caused, not by volcanic activity or enemy saboteurs, but by an airlock at one of the intakes to the tunnel.

During the past two hundred years rescuers have been called out to search the mountain on countless occasions. In the nineteenth century, volunteers armed only with lanterns braved the snowy slopes in search of missing climbers. Even today, with modern mountain rescue equipment, trained tracker dogs, infra-red lenses and helicopters, these intrepid men and women risk their own lives on a regular basis.

Unfortunately, over the years, their job has been made doubly difficult by a number of false alarms. During the winter of 1952 the Lochaber Mountaineering Club were asked to assist in the search for a missing French student from The University of Edinburgh, who had not returned to her digs after telling friends she intended to climb Ben Nevis. The conditions on the mountainside were appalling at the time and the club were unable to mount a search on such vague information. Indeed, there was no proof that the missing lady had even travelled to Fort William. The following year, however, a much more dangerous and tragic search was undertaken by volunteers.

Two experienced climbers from England, Peter Drummond-Smith and David Munro, were reported missing in March 1953, when they did not return from a climbing trip to the mountain. A team of volunteers, together with RAF Mountain Rescue, searched the mountainside for a period of six weeks, looking in vain for the missing climbers. In appalling weather, battling blinding blizzards, with 100 mph winds and 15-foot drifts, the team were twice forced to abandon the search as avalanches and snowstorms threatened their safety. Finally, on 20th April, a grim discovery was made. Two local searchers, Alexander McKellaig a schoolteacher from Fort William, and James Wynne a factory worker from Inverlochy, equipped with 15-foot steel poles to probe the huge snow drifts, found the bodies of the two missing climbers. Still roped together and frozen in anguish, the corpses were located at the foot of the South Castle Gully, more than 3,000 feet from the base. Stretcher parties were despatched the following day to recover the bodies and return them to their families.

Yet, even with the advent of 'walkie-talkie' radios, more sophisticated equipment, and powerful electric torches, the second half of the twentieth century would still see mankind unable to provide answers to all of the mysteries and unanswered questions posed by the ominous presence of Britain's highest mountain.

MOUNTAIN MYSTERIES
(PART TWO)

Air Ministry officials were both alarmed and perplexed in February 1964 when scores of residents in the Laggan Dam and Spean Bridge area reported hearing an aeroplane circling over Ben Nevis for two hours during the dead of night. At the height of Cold War paranoia, the Air Ministry was on high alert for any suspicious activity. Who would possibly risk such a dangerous flight in the pitch black of a winter's night? A 17-man RAF Mountain Rescue Team, under the command of Flying Officer Holt, was despatched to Fort William the following morning. Despite a thorough search, no wreckage was ever found, no recorded flight plan logged with the Air Registration Board (now the Civil Aviation Authority), nor any civilian or military aircraft reported missing.

In December 1972, a 20-strong rescue team, complete with tracker dogs, was despatched to the slopes of Ben Nevis, following the sighting of a distress flare which lit up the mountainside. The rescuers battled blinding snow and 6-foot drifts, managing to reach the rescue hut, located at a height of 2,000 feet. Eventually, after risking life and limb, they were forced to turn back as darkness fell and the weather closed in. On returning to the safety of Fort William they were informed by a helpful local astronomer that the distress 'flare' was, in fact, a shooting star! Apparently, a unique combination of snow, the light level, and the resulting reflections had created the illusion that a distress flare had actually been fired from the surface of the mountain.

Even in the modern era the enigmatic mountain still seems reluctant to provide easy answers to the many questions our interaction with it has raised. In January 1983 two Irish youths went missing during a climb on Ben Nevis. Despite an extensive search, the bodies were not discovered until seven months later, this time by a lone climber in Coire na Ciste, on the north face of the mountain. So inaccessible was the location that no examination of the bodies was possible until a RAF helicopter was able to lower the police and forensic teams into the area.

Ben Nevis revealed a rather unusual musical mystery in May 2006 when volunteers clearing stones from the peak were astonished to unearth a piano near the summit. The piano was recovered by 15 volunteers from the John Muir Trust, the conservation charity which owns part of Ben Nevis. The strange discovery left the volunteers dumbfounded:

Our guys couldn't believe their eyes,' said Trust director Nigel Hawkins, *'At first we thought it was just the wooden casing but then they saw the whole cast iron frame complete with strings. The only thing that that was missing was the keyboard - and that's another mystery. Maybe it's hidden somewhere else on the mountain.*

It was thought that the mystery was solved the following day when a Scots woodcutter revealed that he had carried the instrument up the mountain in 1971 as a charity fundraiser. Kenny Campbell, from Bonar Bridge, spent four days carting what was in fact a church organ to the summit. However, another layer to the riddle was added shortly afterwards when it was revealed that a biscuit wrapper with a 'best before' date of 1986 was discovered underneath the piano – meaning that it must have been placed there long after 1971. The instrument was also confirmed to be a piano and not an organ. In fact, it transpired that a piano had been hauled up the mountain during the summer of 1986, by a group of removal men from Dundee who were hoping to raise money for charity. After conquering the mountain with the 350kg instrument, Mike Clark and his friends celebrated their achievement at the summit with a bottle of whisky and a packet of McVitie's biscuits.

The group confirmed that the instrument they hauled to the mountain top was definitely a piano, meaning that Kenny Campbell's electric organ must still be hidden somewhere near the summit!

On 12th February 2015 several groups of climbers on Ben Nevis were startled to hear what they described as a 'blood-curdling scream' coming from somewhere towards the summit of the mountain. They were not able to locate anything visually, due to heavy cloud, but so convinced were they that someone was in terrible trouble that at least one group of mountaineers abandoned their climb to investigate the scream. After a long search they were unable to locate the source of the terrifying scream and the mountain descended into an eerie silence. Meanwhile, close by, another team of climbers heard, 'an unmistakeable yell or cry for help' and called the emergency services. The Lochaber Mountain Rescue Team were despatched immediately to investigate. They too could not locate the source of the scream.

Later that day, the various climbing groups and clubs on the internet began to compare notes on a climber's forum webpage. It transpired that several different groups had heard the scream, despite being on different parts of the mountain, yet no one had been able to pinpoint the source.

The consensus of opinion from the climbers was of a series of sustained and horrific screams that seemed to last for four or five minutes, before ending abruptly. This was followed by the distinct sound of a woman crying. Some of the climbers also thought they had heard someone call out for a 'tight rope' just before the scream. One of the climbers, Christopher Sleight, later wrote, 'my first thought was simple but terrible: I was listening to someone who had just watched a loved one - not simply a climbing partner, but a loved one - fall to their death. There was so much pain and loss in that dreadful noise.'

However, none of the investigators were able to find any evidence of an accident, nor were there any reports of missing climbers filed with the authorities.

Shortly after the event, the BBC News website posted an article by climber Christopher Sleight, describing the mysterious screams. The BBC website was then flooded with a series of claims either implying, or directly stating, that the screams were of a supernatural origin. The most common suggestions were of a ghost, a banshee (a phantom woman that cries out before a person dies), or the legendary Big Grey Man (the spirit or creature thought to be haunting the peak of Ben Macdui, although the phenomenon had never before been reported on Ben Nevis). The climbers who actually heard the screams, however, all came to the conclusion that the most likely source of the mystery was a panicked wife or girlfriend, who genuinely believed something terrible had happened to their partner, only to be mistaken, and then too embarrassed to admit to being the source of the screams.

There is one mystery that dates back much further, however. Archaeologists have made several trips to an ancient Iron Age hillfort in the shadows of Ben Nevis in an attempt to unravel the mystery surrounding its construction. The 2,500-year-old settlement called Dun Deardail, a hilltop fort on an elevated rocky knoll on the west side of Glen Nevis, probably served as a Celtic fort and then a Pictish citadel.

Even today, its mysterious method of construction continues to defy explanation. The hillfort was originally constructed from stone and timber, which was then burnt at such intense heat that the rocks melted and fused together in a process known as vitrification. Theories on just how the inhabitants were able to create such high temperatures - around 1,000 degrees Celsius - over long periods have divided opinion among archaeologists and geologists (and conspiracy theorists!), all of whom are

keen to find an answer to the
riddle. Archaeologists returned
to Dun Deardail again in
2016. The hillfort is one of 60
vitrified forts in Scotland - with
others including Tap O' North
in Aberdeenshire and Ord
Hill near Inverness. Similar
structures can also be found
in parts of France, Germany,
Wales, Ireland and even Peru.

One theory is that vitrification was a status symbol, marking
the settlement out from other less important forts. Others
believe that a settlement would be set alight by attackers
and inadvertently vitrified in the process. Several historians
have theorised that the process was merely a structural tool
used to strengthen the walls of the fort.

With no clear answer, conspiracy theorists also have their
own views. Science fiction writer and inventor Arthur C
Clark took an interest in Scottish vitrified forts and visited
the site at Dun Deardail during the early 1980s, helping
to recreate an earlier experiment with archaeologist Dr
Ian Ralston. A rampart wall of stone and timber beams was
constructed, with approximately six tons of wood placed
on top, and then burnt for more than 22 hours. Although
some vitrification did take place, the test could not explain
how the process would work successfully on a much larger
structure, such as a fort, nor how such large amounts
of fuel could be transported to a hilltop two and a half
millennia ago.

When asked in 2004 what he considered to be the most intriguing unsolved mystery he had uncovered during his long career, Arthur C Clarke stated: 'The oddest thing is these vitrified forts in Scotland. I just thought, how? After all, lasers were not common in the Stone Age!'

Even today, with all our modern technology and advantages, the lure of conquering the mysterious mountain still claims many lives. Tragic accidents have taken many lives in recent years, usually averaging around five or six deaths every twelve months, with several recorded over the winter of 2019/20 and one climber plunging more than 1,000 feet to his death in March 2022. Yet the number of climbers ascending Ben Nevis seems to increase every year, with the total now averaging around 160,000 per annum, some wearing just training shoes and T-shirts! The threats are manyfold, including sudden and dramatic changes in weather, avalanches, steep slopes, heart attacks, and overhanging snow ledges. Yet the mystery of Britain's largest mountain remains an irresistible lure.

However, of all the many unexplained and tragic stories to occur on the majestic and daunting slopes of Ben Nevis, perhaps the darkest and most sinister of all is the comparatively recent tale of Mr Howard Keeley.

In 2003, a 51-year-old former pupil of Balgowan Approved School in Dundee walked into a police station in Cumbernauld, North Lanarkshire, and told officers Mr Keeley had not died in an accident on the slopes of Ben Nevis in 1962 but had in fact been pushed to his death by two of his pupils, who had literally kicked him over the mountain's edge. The man went on to claim he had been present during the terrible deed and had helped to cover up the horrific event for the past 40 years. Explaining that he could no longer live with his conscience, he had decided to confess to the police. Under questioning he gave the police the names of two other former pupils and revealed the shocking story for the first time.

On the last weekend in February 1962 a group of pupils from the Balgowan School had departed on an expedition to climb Ben Nevis, accompanied by the deputy head, Thomas Jack, and a 23-year-old student volunteer teacher, Howard 'Tim' Keeley.

On the Sunday evening a phone call was made by Mr Jack, the deputy head, to the school's headmaster in Dundee. He reported the horrific news that Mr Keeley was dead, killed in an accidental fall from the north face of the mountain as he led a small group of boys to the summit. The headmaster, Mr Dryden, was shocked to the core. Mr Keeley had been an experienced climber. Suddenly, 40 years on, the forgotten climbing tragedy had become one of Scotland's biggest murder mysteries.

'At the time of the tragedy there was never any question of foul play. The story the boys had given was accepted at face value,' reported Mr Dryden, 'It was an extremely plausible story.'

The schoolboys had given the following description to police in 1962:

We had split into two groups to make the climb, with Mr Keeley and three or four pupils taking the lead. When we reached a height of 3,000ft, near the steep ledge of Coire Leis, one the boys dropped his ice axe. Mr Keeley told us to stay where we were; and he went to retrieve it. He slipped and hit a boulder, then disappeared over the edge. A climber ran back down the track to alert Mr Jack and he led us back to Glen Nevis.

A rescue team later found Mr Keeley's body in a gully, 1,000ft down the mountainside. The boys were questioned at length by police, with Mr Keeley's death eventually declared as an accident.

Balgowan, a residential school, catered for around 100 boys aged 10 to 15, who were classified (at that time) under the label 'juvenile delinquents'. The police launched a complex and frustrating murder investigation. There were no surviving records, many of the witnesses were dead, or had changed their names and could not be traced. Frustratingly, Mr Jack the deputy head of the school and the only other adult present at the time of the tragedy, had died many years earlier and had told the Fort William police at the time that he had not actually witnessed the incident. In addition to this setback, Mr Keeley, the victim of the tragedy, was an only child and his few remaining family members were unable to shed any further light on the mysterious events.

No official documentation from the original investigation could be traced at police headquarters. Detectives then decided to visit the school, in the hope of scrutinising their records, only to discover that Balgowan school had closed in 1983 and had been demolished shortly afterwards, including a classroom named the 'Mr Keeley Room' – dedicated to the memory of the teacher.

Ultimately, the authorities were unable to locate any new information which would have enabled them to overturn the original Coroner's verdict of accident death.

Finally, after eventually tracing and interviewing several former pupils of the school as far away as Australia and South America, the 51-year-old man who had walked into the police station, claiming that the accident was a deliberate murder, was charged with wasting police time.

Despite the police force's best efforts, the family of Howard Keeley remained unsatisfied; claiming that justice was 'still to be done in the case', and that they had always been 'perplexed by the story of "an accident" involving such an experienced and popular climber.'

It seems that the baffling tale of Howard Keeley can be added to the long list of strange and mysterious stories associated with Britain's highest mountain.

WHO KILLED
CATHERINE MACLELLAN?

Of all the stories contained in this book, the tragic tale of
Catherine Gillies is perhaps the saddest. In our cossetted,
modern world of luxury and convenience it is sometimes
hard for us to comprehend just how difficult life must have
been 200 years ago, particularly among the poorer classes.
Even more so if you suffered from any form of mental
illness.

Despite the tragedy of the circumstances, this story gives us
a unique insight into the law, language, social values, and
attitudes among the poorer classes in the Highlands.

Archibald Maclellan had been born in 1799 and was one
of a large number of Maclellans then living as tenants in
a remote spot, approximately eight miles east of Mallaig,
called Kylesmorar Farm, in the parish of Glenelg, close to
the shores of Loch Nevis.

Archibald had married Catherine Gillies when he was
around the age of 20 and the couple had settled at
Kylesmorar, where they grafted out an existence as crofters.
It was a hard life, with few luxuries. Catherine gave birth to

four children and initially the marriage had been a happy
one. However, after six years their relationship had begun
to show signs of strain. Catherine would often forget to feed
the children and was sometimes accused of striking them
in fits of uncontrollable anger. Sometimes she became
so violent that the neighbours overheard her screaming
or destroying furniture. Archibald was frequently forced
to restrain her by binding her hands together with rope.
When this was not effective, he began to tie her to heavy
furniture or to a post, sometimes for 24 hours at a time.
A neighbour even helped him on one occasion. As the
weeks and months passed by, Catherine took to aimlessly
wandering the countryside around the parishes of Arisaig
and Morar, apparently barefoot, and in all weathers. The
duration of her absences from home became longer and
longer. Neighbours often received a knock on the door
during the night, to find a barefoot Catherine begging for
food and a bed for a night.

Her periods away from home became the rule rather than the exception, so much so, that Archibald Maclellan was rumoured to have invited another woman to live with him during his wife's long absences. Mary Gillies, from Ardnamurchan in Glenelg and a distant relative of Catherine's, was seen leaving Maclellan's house late at night and, one witness would later state, 'It was understood in the village that there was an illicit connection betwixt Maclellan and Mary Gillies'.

Late on the evening of Thursday 24th June 1830, Donald Maclellan, another tenant at Kylesmorar, received a knock on the door of his croft. It was a barefooted Catherine Maclellan. She asked for some food, and Donald Maclellan and his wife invited her to stay for supper. After they had finished eating Catherine became fractious and begged to stay the night. She explained to the couple that she feared her husband and did not wish to ever return home. Donald Maclellan told her that she should go home and, despite protesting, Catherine reluctantly did so.

The following morning, Friday 25th June, (the day that King George IV passed away), another tenant at Kylesmorar, John Maclellan, was walking close to the shores of Loch Nevis when he observed Catherine's husband, Archibald, walking away from the shore in an eastward direction. In the delightful language of the time, John Maclellan described Archibald Maclellan as being 'about three or four gunshots' from the rocky shore (a 'gunshot' was the distance at which a shot could be expected to travel, roughly 50-100 yards). After the two men spoke, Archibald changed direction and walked towards his cottage.

Later that day, around 8 o'clock in the evening, John Gillies
and John Maclellan were walking close to the shoreline
between Tarbet and Kylesmorar, at a point where the
marshy land meets the water, when they noticed what
appeared to be a dead body lying on the rocks at the
waters' edge. As they approached they quickly realised it
was the body of Catherine Maclellan. She was slumped
on the ground, still barefoot, with her hands raised, as if
attempting to cover her head. The men observed a large
contusion above her right eyebrow, from which blood had
oozed over her face. A woollen cloth covered her neck
and throat. They decided to move the body above the
waterline, as the sea loch was tidal at that point; and they
didn't want the rising tide to wash her corpse away. As they
did so, they noticed vivid marks around the victim's throat,
which seemed to correspond with a stranglehold grip, and
several cuts and abrasions on her arms and legs. On the
softer ground near the base of the rocks, there appeared
to be drag marks that seemed to indicate that the body had
been hauled down the slope towards the shoreline. At the
top of the rocks they also noticed three pieces of cloth, all
of printed cotton, which had apparently been torn from
Catherine's dress and cap and become snagged on a jagged
piece of stone.

After John Gillies and John Maclellan had moved the body
to a drier and safer position, they rushed to fetch a boat,
so the body could be relocated to her home. It had been
a wild and stormy day and the tidal nature of the loch
could raise the water level by as much as 15 feet. They
then proceeded to tell Archibald Maclellan that they had

discovered his wife's body.

Archibald Maclellan had been working in a potato field about half a mile from the scene of the murder. When the two men broke the devastating news to him, he threw himself to the ground and shook violently, although he remained silent.

The body of Catherine Maclellan was removed by boat and taken along the shore to Archibald Maclellan's house. Several neighbours kept watch over the body on both the Friday and Saturday night while a coffin was created. On the Sunday morning, Catherine was taken to the burial place at Kinloch Nevis.

Many of the locals were suspicious of Archibald Maclellan's part in his wife's death and he was immediately confronted by Duncan Gillies, servant to the landowner John Gillies, 'It is not agreeable what I have seen. What is the meaning of this? Something wrong has been done'. Maclellan replied, 'If I am suspected of this, I will take myself out of it!'

John Gillies, as landowner, took it upon himself to charge Archibald Maclellan with the killing of his wife and immediately sent communication to the Sheriff in Fort William, who in turn despatched his officer, John Campbell, to arrest Maclellan. In the meantime, the Sheriff also requested a surgeon to examine the body of Catherine. John Campbell arrived at Kylesmorar only to find that Maclellan had fled. However, he was quickly apprehended in Tarbet, about two miles away, and placed in a prison cell while the matter was investigated.

Such was the resolve and determination of Kylesmorar's inhabitants to see justice done, that they made the arduous trek to Ardnafour (Arisaig) to provide witness statements against Archibald Maclellan. In 1830 their journey would have taken many hours and involved either a long journey over land or a boat voyage along the sea lochs and coastline.

In the presence of Robert Flyter, the Sheriff Substitute for Fort William, their precognition statements were taken orally in Gaelic (under Scots Law) and later transcribed into English. The Sheriff made the decision that the evidence against Archibald Maclellan warranted a trial and he was charged accordingly (the indictment also included an earlier second offence):

Archibald Maclellan, tenant in Kylesmorar, you are guilty of the crime of murder, actor or part. Insofar as on the 25th day of June eighteen hundred and thirty, on or near that part of the sea-shore, where the march (land between two borders) *between the farm of Kylesmorar aforesaid, and the farm of Ardnamurchan, in the parish of Glenelg, meets the sea, or on or near a rock jutting into the sea at the said part of the sea-shore of Lochnevis, violently, wickedly, and feloniously attacked and assaulted Catherine Gillies or Maclellan your wife, who has for two years, or thereby, wandered through the country and occasionally resided with you, at Kylesmorar aforesaid, and did, with a sharp stone or other sharp and lethal instrument, strike her several severe blows on the head, neck and body, by which she was felled to the ground, and severely cut and injured, and while lying there, you did spring upon her, and did seize her throat with your hands, and violently compress her throat, by which she was strangled, or nearly strangled, and did*

drag her in that state along the ground, and throw her into the sea
from the said shore or from the said rock, where, if any life remained
in her body, she was drowned.

Archibald Maclellan was also charged with attempted
murder:

Also, having previously evinced (publicly revealed) *deadly*
malice and hatred against your wife for twelve months preceding
her death, and with attempting to murder her on the 22ᵐᵈ of June
last, by forcibly holding her head under the water, in a burn at
Kylesmorar.

Archibald Maclellan emphatically pled 'not guilty'.

The case appeared before the Circuit Court in Inverness
during September of 1830. Lord Meadowbank presided. In
all, 24 witnesses were brought forward by the prosecution,
led by Mr A Alison the Advocate Depute. Mr C MacDougal
acted for the defence.

Various witnesses at the trial spoke at length regarding
Archibald Maclellan's previous treatment of his wife. Mary
Kelly testified that she had witnessed the accused 'ill use his
wife; beat her and pitch her on the stones when she was far
gone with child. I saw him put her head in a tub of water
when she was washing.' Mary Kelly also deponed that she
had seen Mary Gillies on the bed of the accused 'while his
wife was not there'.

Margaret MacDonald stated she had overheard Archibald
Maclellan tying his wife and beating her. Another witness
claimed that they had overheard the prisoner say, 'he would
drown his wife if she did not leave him'.

On the day of Catherine's death several witnesses, when questioned, pointed to the fact that Maclellan was spotted close to the scene of the tragedy, walking in the opposite direction. Another witness. Archibald Gillies, stated that he had asked the defendant, 'how did your wife meet her death?' To which Maclellan replied 'God knows!' He then asked for some wood to construct a coffin for his wife. The presence of a large indentation in the ground also appeared to indicate that a large stone had recently been removed, perhaps suggesting a possible murder weapon.

The medical evidence, given by Charles Crichton, the examining practitioner, was inconclusive. It was not clear whether death had occurred by strangulation or had been caused by the blow (or blows) to the head. Neither was Dr Crichton certain that the trauma to Catherine's skull had been caused by a murderous attack or by the action of the sea dashing her head against the sharp rocks that lay on the shoreline as it had been a stormy day and the waters had been rough. In addition, although the scratches and marks to her body were recent, it was impossible to state whether they had occurred on the day of her death.

The defence raised an objection regarding the qualifications of the medical witness and to the second charge of attempted murder, claiming that there were so many burns running into Loch Nevis it would be impossible to pinpoint the exact one in which the offence took place. This was overruled by the judge, however. There was also a problem translating much of the witness evidence from Gaelic into English for the benefit of the legal teams and jury.

Archibald Maclellan, as the accused, was not allowed to speak in his own defence during the trial. His own defence solicitor described him as 'lowly and uneducated' during his summing up. Instead, the Clerk of the Court read Maclellan's pre-prepared written statement aloud to the court. The statement simply stated that Maclellan was innocent and had 'not the slightest idea what may have happened to my poor Catherine.'

Lord Meadowbank summed up the evidence for the jury, stating that although he had formed the opinion that:

The woman had died by external violence, a violence not committed by her own hand. This was proved by the marks on the ground, by the fragments of dress left where the apparent struggle had taken place, and by the appearance of the body.

He regretted that better medical evidence was not possible; but warned the jury that they must only convict if they were certain beyond all reasonable doubt of the prisoner's guilt. The question of Maclellan's previous treatment of his wife was also raised. To quote Lord Meadowbank: 'It was proved that the deceased was insane, and occasionally troublesome and vexed, therefore it must be considered whether the prisoner might have used all the coercive measure charged against him, such as tying her hands and confining her, without meaning violence'

(It must be remembered that, whilst abhorrent to our modern sensibilities, there was little understanding of mental illness in 1830 and the methods used by Archibald Maclellan was a common 'treatment' at the time).

The jury retired, and after deliberating for only fifteen minutes, returned a unanimous verdict of 'not proven'. The prisoner was visibly relieved as he left the court a free man.

So, why did Archibald Maclellan walk away a free man (if not, without a stain on his character)?

Firstly, Scottish juries were notoriously reluctant to condemn a man to death when the 'not proven' verdict was available to them (this anomaly has also been discussed in my previous books *The River Runs Red* and *Blood Beneath Ben Nevis*). There were far fewer cases of the death penalty being imposed in Scotland, during the 18th and 19th centuries, than in neighbouring England.

Secondly, it appeared that the witnesses were largely convinced of Maclellan's guilt, purely based on his previous behaviour towards his wife, and not the actual evidence available on the day of the crime. The witnesses' evidence was then clearly taken by the jury as being highly biased. For instance, the timings given by them were confidently precise, yet it was unlikely any of the witnesses had access to a pocket-watch, or even a clock in their humble cottages.

Was Archibald Maclellan guilty? We will probably never know; however, other explanations are highly plausible. The affair between Archibald Maclellan and Mary Gillies was common knowledge among the other inhabitants at Kylesmorar. Whilst Mary Gillies was not on trial, she, at least, had as legitimate a motive for the death of Catherine Maclellan, as Archibald Maclellan did. Yet she was not even called as a witness, by either side, in court. She was a widow and shortly before the murder had moved to nearby Ardnamurchan. It also appears that Maclellan may have been heading towards her new home on both the day of the crime, and on the day of his arrest.

The question of Catherine Maclellan's mental illness was never examined or proved, just assumed, based on the statements from the witnesses. It is impossible for us now to diagnose her mental state; however, many of the circumstances relating to her death might well be explained as suicide, or misadventure today. Her husband's reprehensible treatment of her, whilst horrifying to our modern sensibilities, was not uncommon at the time. Indeed, fear and distrust of mentally ill patients may well have garnered some sympathy for Archibald Maclellan from the members of the jury. Fears that his four children would be left homeless, with their father in prison and their mother dead, may also have played into Maclellan's hands.

If Maclellan had deliberately planned to kill his wife, the location at which the crime took place also seems an odd one. Maclellan could have easily taken Catherine's body out into the loch on his boat, where it would have washed out seaward, or found a spot where the rocks on the shoreline would not have snagged the body, thereby keeping it close to the land. After all, he had lived in the area all his life and knew the waters well.

And what became of Archibald Maclellan and his lover Mary Gillies?

Mary Gillies, it appears, returned to her cottage in Kinlochmorar and lived out her days as a respectable widow. It is hard to imagine that she would have been welcomed at Kylesmorar and probably had little reason to visit, following the humiliation of the trial.

The 'not proven' verdict carries with it a certain stigma. Especially for Archibald Maclellan in such a closely knit community, where everyone clearly believed he had both murdered his wife and also carried on an illicit affair with Mary Gillies. It appears that he did not remain in the area. The early parish records for the area (mostly undertaken by the church or by schoolmasters during the 1830s) list Archibald Maclellan and his family. However, by the time of the 1841 census, Maclellan and his four children seemed to have vanished from the region and cannot be found anywhere on the census records. So, where did they travel to escape the humiliation of the court case and the resulting speculation? The answer to that question has been unanswered for many years. However, in researching this story, I did uncover the most likely solution. There is a record of an Archibald Maclellan, with the same date of birth, emigrating from the west of Scotland to Nova Scotia in Canada. Listing his occupation as 'farmer' he did not travel with a wife; but did have four children. There were a large number of Scots (including many Maclellans) who emigrated to Nova Scotia during the mid-19th century, mainly to escape the clearances and economic hardship, and he could even have had family members already there. If it is the same Archibald Maclellan, which seems highly probable, it seems that he lived a long and satisfying life in his new home, eventually passing away in Richmond, Nova Scotia on 4th March 1874 at the age of 75.

His son James registered his death, citing the cause of his father's death as 'asthma'. I cannot help wondering if any of Maclellan's children could remember their mother; or what story of their mother's death they grew up believing.

FORT WILLIAM'S DARKEST DAY

For the residents of Fort William, nestled between the slopes of Ben Nevis and the expanse of Loch Linnhe, Wednesday 9th April 1909 may well be remembered as the darkest day in the community's history. A day that started like any other; yet would end in a tragedy that focused unwelcome national attention on Fort William and united the whole town together in anger, grief and sorrow. For many years to follow a veil was cast over the memory and the incident never spoken of, to the extent that the dreadful events of that Wednesday morning have been largely forgotten.

The misty morning of Wednesday 9th April 1909 was much like any other working morning for John Gray. John, aged 39, worked for the North British Railway Company and needed to clock in at Fort William Railway Station by 6am. A likeable, studious, and deeply religious man, John Gray was awake bright and early. He boiled some water on the stove for an early morning cup of tea. He always carried a cup through to his wife Margaret before he left for work. While he waited for the water to heat up, he dressed, shaved (leaving his cut-throat razor next to the sink) and glanced at the previous day's newspaper, still left open on the small wooden table. Making sure not to the wake the couple's children, Robert, aged ten, and Agnes, aged eight, he carefully carried a cup of tea through to Margaret, gently waking her as he did so. John told her that he was going to work, as he had to supervise the early morning train. 'I'll be back about nine o'clock for breakfast', he told her, as he slipped on his jacket. She seemed cheerier than of late, he thought to himself. Kissing her on the cheek he whispered, 'goodbye'. Margaret answered with a sleepy 'bye'. It would be the last words exchanged by the couple.

Gray put his cap on and, quietly closing the front door, left the family's small cottage in Fassifern Road, heading down the hill, past the chapel, to the railway station by the loch side. The morning was damp and murky, and he turned his collar up, thrusting his hands in his pockets. It was still dark. As he strode along, he passed two workmen walking in the other direction, their heads down so that their caps obscured their faces. Neither of the men acknowledged or spoke to him.

After his morning shift, he returned, as usual, at nine o'clock, for breakfast. It was very much a routine in the Gray household. John would return to their lodging in the cottage about nine o'clock. The stove would be lit and their home warm and welcoming. The children would be up and dressed, either already departed for school, or (as was the case that day) on holiday, but awake, dressed and sat at the table ready to say 'grace' with their father before eating breakfast. The family were members of the

Independent Order of Rechabites, a religious organisation founded in 1835, that adhered faithfully to the principle of total abstinence. The Grays had moved to Fort William from Lorn Street, in Helensburgh, after John had been offered a position with the railway company in the town. He had wanted a change from his previous position as a butter salesman. Bringing their beliefs with them, the family had helped to open a new lodge (known as a 'tent') for the Rechabites in Fort William. John and Margaret Gray were well respected within the town, and their children popular among their playmates. John did not enter the public houses of the town, unlike the other workmen, preferring to stay home and spend time with his family or attending prayer meetings.

It was now light, although still fairly dreary, and John was surprised to see that the windows at the front of the cottage were still in darkness, the curtains drawn. As he entered the front door the narrow passageway of the cottage was still in darkness. The lamps had not yet been lit. He called out, 'Maggie!' As he did so, he became aware of a muffled noise and the slight sound of movement from the back of the house. He removed his cap and jacket, hanging them up in the hallway. Again, he called out, 'Maggie! I'm home'. There was no answer. Gray walked along the narrow passage and glanced into the dimly lit kitchen. The room was in darkness, as he had left it. The table was not laid, breakfast had not been prepared, and the stove not lit. John noticed that his razor had been moved from the windowsill, next to the sink, and that the back door to the yard was now unbolted. He hastily entered the children's bedroom wondering why they were not awake. As he did so, a scene of unimaginable horror confronted him.

Robert and Agnes, the couple's children, shared a bed in the small room. Their bodies were still curled up together, as if asleep, yet their faces appeared contorted with pain and their heads were horribly traumatised by horrific injuries. Seeping from deep wounds on their heads, huge amounts of blood had flowed, covering their entire bodies, bedclothes and bedding in a deep red blanket.

John Gray recoiled in horror; as he did so, he noticed a small, blood-stained hatchet lying on the bed next to their disfigured bodies. He turned his head away from the horrific sight and staggered to the kitchen to sit down. As he did so, Gray became aware that Margaret's body was slumped on the floor in the far corner, her upper torso and the kitchen floor beneath her awash with blood. Next to her body lay the cut-throat razor he had used just a few hours earlier. Blood was still oozing from a deep gash across her throat. Margaret's face and neck were covered in gashes and cuts, and her right hand was tightly clasped across the deep wound on her throat. John rushed to her side and noticed instantly that she was still alive. Crying out her name, he rushed out into the street and shouted out for help. Within minutes, medical help and other assistance arrived, including a police constable from Fort William police station who had been on morning patrol. Margaret Gray was, indeed, still alive – but in a critical state. Her eyes were open and, although in a semi-conscious state, she appeared to be attempting to communicate with those in the room. Time was of the essence, however, and she was rushed to Belford Hospital in the town.

Meanwhile, the news spread rapidly, as speculation and gossip took hold. Was a madman at loose in the town? Had Margaret Gray killed her own children, then tried to take her own life?

Initially, Mrs Gray was not expected to live. She drifted in and out of consciousness and was unable to speak. Such were the levels of ill feeling towards her in the community

that an armed and continuous police guard was placed around her hospital bed, perhaps for the only time in Fort William's history. She was visited in the afternoon by Sheriff Davidson, Mr A Mackenzie (the Depute Procurator-Fiscal), Inspector Chisholm, and Police Sergeant Mackenzie, with the view, if possible, of obtaining a deposition from her. However, the doctors thought that the trauma caused by such a line of questioning would prevent any chance of recovery. Inspector Chisholm reluctantly agreed, realising that the police would be powerless to charge her with the murder of her children until such time as they were able to question her. Meanwhile crowds gathered outside, chanting and baying for justice.

Meanwhile John Gray, and any potential witnesses, were questioned at length:

Where did the hatchet used to kill the children come from, Mr Gray.

It was kept in an outhouse, I used it for chopping wood.

Was the outhouse locked?

Er, no.

So, Mrs Gray, or the children, could have access to it at any time.

Yes, I suppose so, but Robert and Agnes knew they were not allowed to play with it.

So, anyone could have taken it?, the officer asked.

Yes sir.

The detective continued, *Was Mrs Gray sound in her mind? Our inquiries tell us that she had been somewhat depressed of late.*

Aye, she was not good over the winter. But nothing like this! In fact, she had been much better recently. She loved Robert and Agnes more than anything in the world.

And she was a religious woman?

Aye. We both are.

The neighbours were questioned too. They all confirmed that Mrs Gray was a devoted mother and loved her children dearly. No one had ever heard a cross word or a raised voice coming from their house. Two tradesmen working in an adjoining house were able to tell the police that they had not heard any disturbance or suspicious sound emanating from the Gray's house on the morning of the murder. Due to the early morning half-light, however, John Gray was not able to confirm that these were the two workmen he had seen at 6am on the day of the murder as he left for work. Gray firmly believed that his wife could not have killed her own children; and protested in an animated fashion to the police that they investigate another line of enquiry,

'What about the two men I saw?' he exclaimed. 'You must look for them! They must have done this thing.'

Three days later, the funeral of Robert and Agnes Gray took place outside the Belford Hospital. The service was conducted in the open air at the hospital by Rev R Crawford from Kilmallie, and the Rev John Macintosh from Fort William. The church bells tolled as a sombre atmosphere enveloped the town. Evidence of the community's sympathy was clear. An exceptionally large audience gathered at the service, including members of the Boys' Brigade, who led the melancholy procession, the Girls' Guild, and the Rechabites. The two small white coffins were placed in an open hearse and covered with floral tributes. As the sombre cortege passed through Fort William, on its way to the railway station, all business in the town was suspended entirely, and the blinds in private dwellings drawn as a mark of respect. The bodies of the children were to be taken to Helensburgh to be buried alongside their father's family

Contrary to the doctor's expectations Margaret Gray's condition improved after a few days and the police felt confident that she would soon be strong enough to answer some questions. Despite her slight improvement, however, she was still unable to talk and, it appeared, carried no memory of the tragic events. This, it transpired, was to be a false dawn. Margaret Gray developed a sepsis blood infection and lapsed back into a state of unconsciousness, from which she never recovered. It is likely that her weakened immune system, coupled with the trauma of the awful events, was simply too much for her. Margaret Gray passed away on Tuesday 18th May, five weeks after the death of her much-loved children. Despite a policeman being present at her bedside for the entire length of her time in hospital, she was never able to speak coherently or remember the events of that morning.

In a marked contrast to her children, Margaret's body was taken away in secrecy and buried in an unmarked grave, to avoid any ugly scenes or attempts by the public to desecrate her final resting place.

John Gray was never able to recover from the events and, despite much local sympathy and support, left Fort William shortly afterwards, never to return. He initially moved back to his family home in Dunbartonshire and never spoke of his experiences again. Following the Great War, he emigrated to the Transvaal in South Africa, where he remained for the rest of his life, until passing away in 1948 at the age of 78. He went to his grave still believing that his wife could not have killed their children.

The police closed the case on the tragic deaths of Robert and Agnes Gray. It was decided that Margaret Gray had committed the gruesome act. Her actions were accounted for as 'sudden mental derangement'. Despite John Gray's firm belief that his wife could never have murdered her children, and the shocking nature of the incident, no further lines of inquiry were pursued. No one other witness ever came forward to confirm the identity of the two men who had passed John Gray in the street on the morning of the frenzied attack.

Had Margaret Gray really committed such a horrific act, so suddenly, and so utterly out of character? The police certainly believed so. She had been known to have suffered from lapses of depression, or 'black moods', and was said to have lately been in 'a state of poor health'. Yet there was nothing in her past actions to suggest anything of this magnitude was even a remote possibility.

As for the hatchet kept in the outhouse, if Margaret Gray did use it to kill her own children, why did she not attempt to kill herself with the same weapon? Perhaps she did, but it was too cumbersome, meaning that she resorted to the razor so handily placed?

Several questions were not asked. If she was in a deranged mental state with no apparent memory of anything that transpired that morning, how did she have the foresight to go outside to the outhouse, find the hatchet, return to the house (remembering to close both doors), then begin her murderous assault? Why did she not simply use the cut-throat razor, so easily to hand? The question of a third person being present was never seriously entertained or investigated. Yet, it would have been just as easy for someone else to have entered through the rear door, which was unlocked, collecting the hatchet from the outhouse on the way. Perhaps with the intention of robbing the house, after seeing the husband leaving for work. It was impossible to ascertain how much time had passed between the death of the children and the injuries to Mrs Gray. Nor was an exact time of death recorded, which could have feasibly taken place at any point between 6am and just before 9am.

Another point, which does not seem to have been mentioned in the investigation, is the question of the children. Judging by their position in the bed, they were apparently still asleep at the moment they met their death. Would an intruder, if indeed an intruder had entered the house at all, still choose to commit so brutal a crime if the children were still asleep? Perhaps the children had stirred briefly, and the killer simply panicked, or the bodies had been placed back on the bed to give the appearance of sleeping? Sadly, there is no conclusive answer to this important question.

Mrs Gray's previous behaviour had been exemplary, certainly nothing that would have caused any concern to her husband or anyone that knew her. The attack on the children was a genuine surprise, completely out of character, and not something that had ever crossed the mind of John Gray. The case certainly caused a great deal of pain, distress, and soul-searching to the local community, who were happy to see the matter laid to rest quickly. With the victims all buried elsewhere, and the Independent

Order of Rechabites relocating shortly afterwards, little remained to remind the townsfolk of Fort William of the tragic events.

One crucial point, however, may have been missed at the time. When questioned by the police, John Gray told the detectives that he had the distinct impression he had heard a noise from the back of the house as he had entered through the front door, on that fateful morning. Was that noise the sound of an intruder, interrupted in their gruesome act, hastily leaving via the back door? Or was it simply a last vain attempt by Margaret Gray to cry out in tortured anguish? We will never know.

THE POACHER
AND THE POLICEMAN

It was five days before Christmas, on a cold Tuesday, during the winter of 1898. Police Constable Thomas King, an officer with 15 years' experience, had been issued with an arrest warrant to detain a notorious poacher in the village of Nethy Bridge, close to the River Spey. PC King bid farewell to his wife Jessie and their eight children, as they excitedly discussed the family's preparations for Christmas, in front of the open fire. He closed the door and left the police house. It would be the last time his family would see him alive.

The story begins, however, many years earlier in the Braes of Lochaber.

Allan MacCallum was a reckless and fearless poacher, the most notorious in Lochaber and probably the whole of the Highlands. His flagrant disregard for authority, his volatile temper, and his stubborn nature made him a dangerous man to cross.

Originally born at Loch Ericht in Perthshire, MacCallum's family moved to the Braes of Lochaber when he was still a boy. His father was a gamekeeper in the employment of an English gentleman sportsman who owned a large estate close to Fort William. Given the freedom to roam almost feral as child, MacCallum began his career in poaching. As he grew older, he became more and more reckless; and his parents became ever more worried. Ferocious arguments were commonplace, often involving aggrieved landowners. His mother and father, popular members of the Nether Lochaber congregation, despaired for him.

Eventually, following his father's death, MacCallum's mother moved him to various locations around the Highlands, hoping they could settle and start afresh. But MacCallum could not leave his old habits behind and confrontations with gamekeepers and landlords became commonplace. Finally, he was sent away for several years to act as a shepherd on the Falkland Islands.

MacCallum returned to the Highlands of Scotland in 1890, now aged 37. He eventually settled with his mother and brother in Coylumbridge, close to Aviemore. However, this quiet and tranquil location soon became a base for his poaching activities. MacCallum built up a lucrative trade; rapidly becoming one of the most wanted men in the Highlands. Somehow, armed with his shotgun and with his trusted dog for a companion, he managed to stay one step ahead of the police and the angry landowners, usually due to his acute knowledge of the countryside. He often favoured locations close to rural railway stations, such as Boat of Garten or Roy Bridge, from where he could despatch his consignments of illegal game. The hunt for MacCallum regularly featured in the Scottish newspapers:

No poacher had better opportunities for prosecuting his illegal calling than the wild mountainous districts, with their wooded forests, north of the great Grampian chain stretching from Banffshire on the east to Fort William on the west. Allan knew every mile of it, knew the uninhabited bothies in the depths of the forest of Glenmore and the lonely huts on the slopes of the blue ridges of the Cairngorms and in the lowest furrowed ravines of Ben Nevis. He had studied, too, where to get the best markets for his spoil.

MacCallum's brother, Donald, who was a legitimate gamekeeper, objected strongly to his sibling's poaching activities and the pair argued violently, resulting in an attempt by Donald MacCallum to turn his own brother over to the police. However, thanks to his ingenuity, and poacher's instinct, they were unable to catch him.

Gradually, either due the solitude of his existence or to underlying mental health conditions, Allan MacCallum's behaviour became increasingly erratic. The outstanding warrants and unpaid poaching fines began to mount, adding to the pressure and the public's disquiet. Described by the newspapers as 'insane and dangerous', the inhabitants of the Highlands were warned not to approach him. Meanwhile the authorities hatched a plan to capture MacCallum, 'and have him examined by a competent medical authority, who would (they thought) have readily certified that he is not a man that should be allowed to roam at large.'

On the morning of 20th December 1898, PC King set off to exercise the arrest warrant for Allan MacCallum. The two men had crossed paths before, and PC King was only too aware of the danger that MacCallum posed. Mindful that the operation would not be a routine one, PC King had arranged to meet his fellow police officer John MacNiven, who was stationed at Boat of Garten, to help him make the arrest. They believed that MacCallum was, at that time, hiding in a small, wooden, two-bedroomed cottage (known as a 'but and ben' cottage) at the Milton of Tulloch, deep in the woods of Tulloch near Nethybridge. The cottage was occupied by an elderly lady called May MacPherson and her daughter, with whom MacCallum apparently had formed a relationship.

On their arrival in the area, the officers cautiously approached the cottage, located in a clearing among the trees. May MacPherson informed the two officers that MacCallum had been there earlier in the day but had left to collect firewood. The policemen thanked her and left. Believing that the elderly lady was covering for MacCallum they decided to hide among the trees and keep the cottage under observation, awaiting MacCallum's next movement. Ideally, the officers agreed, they would wait for MacCallum to be alone in the building before approaching it, thus ensuring that no-one else would be placed in any danger. MacCallum was undoubtedly armed (he always carried a rifle for use in his poaching activities) and there was little doubt in the officers' minds that he would have no compunction at using a firearm to evade arrest. Used to the outdoor life, MacCallum would undoubtedly do anything he deemed necessary to avoid incarceration.

After a short time, May MacPherson and her daughter were observed scurrying away from the cottage, more than likely in an attempt to try and warn MacCallum about the police officers' visit. PC MacNiven followed her into the surrounding woodland, but lost track of her. PC King, who knew MacCallum by sight, due to their skirmishes in the past, maintained observation on the house. Meanwhile, PC MacNiven was returning to the cottage when MacCallum

jumped out from behind a large tree and pointed his rifle at the police officer. MacCallum shouted a warning to him, 'If you come an inch further I will put this through your heart.' The constable attempted to reason with MacCallum but the wanted man was angry and agitated, 'I suppose you are after me for that fine. I will pay the fine, but, damn, I will fight for my liberty.' For a moment, PC MacNiven thought he was about to be shot, when suddenly MacCallum turned and ran off into the woods, disappearing among the trees. Breathless, and still shaking,

PC MacNiven made his way back to join PC King and warn him.

It was now 4pm and already the light was fading. As they debated their next course of action the officers encountered Mr Grant, the local postman, just on his way back into the village having come from the direction of the cottage. He was able to inform them that he had just witnessed MacCallum entering the cottage.

The two officers decided to approach the cottage before darkness descended. As they did so, PC King - who knew MacCallum fairly well - shouted a greeting to him. No response or reaction came from the cottage. They shouted again. Still no reply. The cottage was in darkness now and there was not a flicker of movement anywhere.

King and MacNiven entered the unlit two-roomed cottage through the porch covered front door. They shouted out 'MacCallum!' again. Their call was met with silence. Inside the cottage it was dingy and dark, with a just a small four-paned window in each of the two rooms. PC King motioned to his colleague that he would search the kitchen (the location he felt MacCallum was more likely to be hiding in) and PC MacNiven was to search the bedroom. MacNiven, on entering the bedroom, heard a loud bang which made him spin around for one terrifying moment, thinking that he had been shot. When he realised he was unhurt, he knew the noise must have come from the kitchen. Rushing in the semi-darkness he tripped over something lying in the kitchen, just inside the doorway. Bending down, and striking a match, he realised it was the body of Constable King, who had been shot in the chest without warning the moment he had entered the kitchen. He had been killed instantly.

A large chest sat in the corner of the kitchen. PC MacNiven nervously opened it, expecting MacCallum to leap out, but it was empty. The room was otherwise bare, MacCallum having obviously escaped from the rear into the thickly wooded land behind the cottage. PC MacNiven, alone and unarmed, returned to the village to fetch Dr Mackay and raise the alarm. The following day PC King's body was removed to his home and to his grieving family. Meanwhile, a full-scale manhunt was launched for MacCallum and his description circulated to all the Scottish newspapers (who embellished it somewhat for the benefit of their readers):

Allan MaCallum is a man about forty-three years of age, of splendid physique, and stands five feet ten or eleven inches high. He is broad-shouldered, deep-chested, with powerful arms and legs. He has a tendency to corpulence, with a slightly bulldog type of neck, but taken all over, a stranger meeting him casually in the Highlands, would set him down as a good specimen of the gamekeeper type. He always wore knickerbockers made of home-spun tweed, heavy thick home-woven stockings, and hobnailed boots. He had a slight moustache, thick darkish hair, and wore frequently a double-peaked Inverness cap. There is nothing in the features that suggests crime or vice although his eyes appear fierce and full of fire. He walks with the slow measured gait peculiar to the gamekeeper, and seems to suspect everyone with whom he comes into contact.

It was assumed that MacCallum would flee the district and try to conceal himself in an area he knew well. Teams of police officers, using tracker dogs, scoured the area around Fort William, Spean Bridge, Roy Bridge, Glen Nevis, Inverroy, the River Spean and Loch Laggan. Mountain huts and cottages were searched but all to no avail. The efforts of the police then turned to the east, with sightings of MacCallum reported in Inverness and Deeside among others. Police were informed that MacCallum had visited a house at Clachaig and obtained food from the terrified owner, Angus Grant. The following day, Friday 30th December, he was spotted at a croft called Tomnachrochar, a mile or two from Clachaig; and just a few miles from where the murder had taken place. The net was closing in. A large contingent of police was despatched to the farmhouse, where MacCallum was discovered, completely hidden under a huge pile of hay in the barns. Such were the overwhelming odds that he surrendered without a struggle. Answering the charge of murder, he simply replied, 'I have nothing to say.' His hands were then bound tightly with rope and he was taken away to await trial.

As MacCallum was being arrested, the funeral of PC Thomas King was taking place in Abernethy Churchyard.

The trial date was set for 14th February 1899 at the Inverness High Court of the Justiciary. Allan MacCallum, who gave his age as 39 (as he was not sure of his actual birth year) had already pleaded not guilty with a special defence plea of insanity at the time of the offence. His brother was asked to send MacCallum a new suit of clothes, so that he might have something presentable to wear for his trial.

In front of a packed courthouse the trial commenced

under presiding judge Lord Trayner. Several witnesses were examined, who all reported seeing MacCallum fleeing the scene of the crime. They all confirmed that he seemed to be of sound mind.

Despite MacCallum's protestations that he had offered to pay the fine when PC King had entered the kitchen, Dr Mackay expressed to the court that he was of the opinion the shot had been fired at close range and was not accidental.

Several expert medical witnesses confirmed their belief that Allan MacCallum was perfectly sane, being capable of understanding the difference between right and wrong. Dr Barclay, from Grantown-on-Spey, revealed to the court that he had been asked to examine MacCallum several years earlier and had concluded that he *was* 'quiet, reserved and sullen, but was responsible for his actions.' Whilst on remand awaiting trial MacCallum was examined several times by the prison doctor. Although MacCallum claimed that 'sunstroke has affected my actions', no evidence was found of this.

The defence claimed that MacCallum had suffered from 'pains in the head' since his return from the Falkland Islands several years earlier; however, this line of defence did not seem to hold much weight with the jury.

After just 15 minutes' deliberation, the jury returned a verdict of guilty to the charge of culpable homicide, but not to murder. There was a gasp of disbelief from the public gallery and, later, from the crowds amassed outside. Lord Trayner, who seems to have adopted a sympathetic approach towards the accused from the outset of the trial, remarked to the court:

Your crime was of a very serious nature indeed. That you took away a man's life no one can doubt. I do not want to aggravate the distressful character of your position upon the present occasion. I think that you had from your counsel and from the jury a most humane consideration, but I am unable to make the sentence less than fifteen years' penal servitude (prison with hard labour).

MacCallum was led away from the courthouse to the prison next door, appearing to the world as a much-relieved man. He served his sentence without incident and was released just prior to the commencement of the Great War.

PC King's widow, Jessie, and his eight children were allowed to continue living in the police house for 'as long as they wished'. However, anxious for a fresh start, the family emigrated to Australia shortly afterwards. Jessie continued to receive her police widow's pension until her death in Brisbane, Queensland, in 1948 at the age of 89.

The family never forgot their Highland heritage. PC King's eldest son (Thomas, junior) became one of the leading figures in Highland dancing in Australia, firstly as a competitor and later a judge in the competitions. He died, aged 94, in a Brisbane Nursing Home in December 1976 and, the following year, his ashes were interred in his father's grave in Abernethy Churchyard.

In 2016, PC King's great-great grandson, Inspector Trevor Gould of the Queensland Police Service, visited the regional police headquarters in Inverness to view the memorial plaque erected for his ancestor.

PC Thomas King was the last police officer to be killed in an act of violence, anywhere in the Highlands of Scotland. His name is also recorded on the Scottish Police Memorial and at the National Memorial Arboretum.

THE GREAT
POST OFFICE ROBBERIES

During the austere latter years of the 1920s, four young men, from very different parts of the United Kingdom, decided to escape the boredom of their daily lives and join the Scots Guards. John MacDonald, Alexander MacRae, John Cook, and Englishman Joseph James.

However, none of the men seemed suited to the army regime and left shortly afterwards. They returned to their respective homes, MacDonald to Portree on the Isle of Skye, MacRae and Cook to Aberdeen, and James to Mansfield in Nottinghamshire. The men vowed to keep in touch and agreed to help each other out, should the occasion arise. They each searched for employment, but each, in turn, found hard work and the monotony of daily routine not to their taste.

John MacDonald became a police constable but was dismissed after twelve months for a 'lack of aptitude'. He returned to the Isle of Skye and married his sweetheart, and before long was the father of two young boys.

Joseph James returned to Mansfield in England, taking

various positions until he found employment at the post
office in the town. Meanwhile, MacRae and Cook took
employment on the railways and contacted MacDonald,
persuading him to do the same. The three men began
as apprentice fitters and mechanics with the London,
Midland, and Scottish Railway Company (LMS), and were
soon enjoying the relative freedom that came with their
new positions. Macdonald, especially, enjoyed the freedom
to travel across the country by rail. He would regularly
leave his home on Syke, cross to Mallaig by ferry, before
spending the week away from home, travelling the length
and breadth of the country with the LMS locomotives.
He spent his weeknights in London, before returning to
Fort William, and then to Skye, at the weekends. During
his time 'on the plate' he witnessed all classes and types of
passenger on the network, from downtrodden farmworkers
to well-heeled businessmen accompanied by rich, upper-
class ladies. It was not long until his good looks attracted
female attention. Unfortunately, his financial situation did
not match his roving eye or his sexual ambitions. However,
he was also blessed with a sharp brain and quick wits; and
before long he hatched a daring plan to rob several of
Britain's post offices – using his knowledge of the railway
network as a means of escape.

By the beginning of 1929 John MacDonald had fine-
tuned his masterplan. Travelling extensively throughout
the country on board the rail network had presented
him with the perfect cover from which he could observe
the high value goods then being transported via Britain's
railways; and also to spot the strengths and weaknesses of

the railway company's security arrangements. In addition, he also considered the important question of a safe getaway. Macdonald soon realised that being able to travel quickly from the scene of a crime by motor car was too risky, with too many potential witnesses likely to notice a suspiciously parked vehicle in the hours leading up to the robbery. Besides, it would require stealing a vehicle in the first place, which was likely to be reported to the police, thus doubling the risk. Breaking into banks, Macdonald concluded, seemed too difficult a task. However, after observing the transfer of cash, treasury bills and registered mail, from post offices onto railway carriages, he concluded that the relatively light security presented him with far easier picking. Getting away with the crime seemed much easier too. MacDonald realised that two opportunities presented themselves. Firstly, he could either break into the goods van while the train was en route, remove items from the mailbags, and alight at another station before the robbery was discovered. Secondly, MacDonald reasoned that he might be able to break into a provincial post office, under cover of darkness. Then, using his railway tools, force an entry into both the premises and safes, before calmly reboarding the next train as a legitimate railway employee, before the theft was discovered. After all, who would suspect a fitter boarding the train in his overalls and carrying his tool bag? The plan seemed perfect. Within a few hours he would be back in Fort William, or hundreds of miles away at the end of the line in London. All that remained was a dry run.

In February 1929 bad weather gave MacDonald his first

opportunity, when working on the overnight mail train from Scotland to London. Post office staff had loaded sacks of mail onto a mail coach at Doncaster. However thick fog had meant that the coach was shunted into sidings to await coupling to a later train. When the train finally arrived at King's Cross at 4.40 am, 54 registered letters were missing. All the letters probably contained cash; however, the true value of theft could never be calculated. What is known, however, is that John MacDonald returned to Fort William, and then to his home on Skye, the following day, without the shadow of suspicion falling upon him. The theft was never solved.

Buoyed by his success, MacDonald contacted his ex-army colleague Joseph James in July 1929, and the pair agreed to attempt a robbery at the Mansfield Post Office, where James was employed at the time. With James' intimate knowledge of the post office's internal procedures, coupled with MacDonald's cleverly planned escape route to Fort William by rail and taxi, the plan seemed foolproof. Firstly, Joseph James left work early on the day of the planned robbery, feigning illness, with £145 belonging to the Postmaster in his jacket pocket. He then met MacDonald at his lodgings in the town. The men planned to journey to Fort William, via Mallaig to Skye, where MacDonald intended to hide James, assuming the police would never consider widening their search parameters as far as the Scottish islands. However, the £145 proceeds (approximately £9,000 today) from the theft disappointed MacDonald, who had hoped for far more. He decided to remain in Mansfield and persuade James that they should adopt the riskier strategy of breaking into the post office that night instead.

So, on the night of Tuesday 20th August 1929, under cover
of darkness, the two men levered open the rear door
into the Post Office. Creeping silently along the corridor,
James was able to direct MacDonald to the sorting office.
Once inside, using the light from a small torch, the two
men forced open the smaller of the three safes. The two
larger safes, which contained large amounts of cash, would
have required substantially more effective hardware than
the tools contained in MacDonald's LMS fitter's tool
bag. This, however, was part of their plan. The small safe
was comparatively easy to jemmy open, which the men
did within a matter of minutes and without creating a

significant amount of noise, which would have no doubt
aroused suspicion from outside.

Within moments the men slipped away through the rear
entrance of the building. James, dressed respectably,
carried the spoils spread evenly across his suit pockets

– the £145 belonging to the Postmaster and a number
of registered packets containing £1,250 in used and
untraceable Treasury Bills. An amount equivalent to
approximately £90,000 today. The men then took separate
routes to Mansfield railway station. MacDonald, dressed in
his LMS overalls, borded the locomotive on the 'up' train
to Scotland, still carrying his toolbag. What could be less
suspicious? He even found time to pass the time of day with
the station master Mr Leech.

It was agreed that James would follow a more circuitous
route, taking a taxi from Mansfield station to Nottingham
(therefore appearing to be a recently alighted train
passenger), before travelling south to Cheltenham, and
eventually taking the LMS express north to Fort William,
where he had arranged to rendezvous with MacDonald and
split their ill-gotten gains. Unfortunately, James handed the
taxi driver a £2 tip – almost £150 today - a act of generosity
which would later be given in evidence against him. Their
seemingly well thought out plan ensured the two men
would not be seen together, meaning they could not be
suspected of working as a team. MacDonald assumed that
Fort William was so remote, that James could easily escape
arrest there.

Regrettably for the two men, the theft was discovered as
soon as the post office opened on Wednesday morning,
and suspicion immediately fell on James, who had, of
course, failed to show up for work. Police and the post
office's own detective staff quickly visited James' lodgings
and, discovering he was not at home, searched his room,
finding his suitcase missing and three paper wrappers, used

to wrap banknotes, partly burnt in the grate. Without any knowledge of his whereabouts, it was decided to urgently issue a description to all police forces and local BBC radio networks within the country. Within a matter of 24 hours, James' description was known to every police force in the land.

Blissfully unaware of this, James arrived in Fort William and walked from the railway station along the High Street where he had arranged to meet MacDonald outside the Alexandra Hotel. Within yards of the hotel, two police constables from Fort William Police Station, John Black and Neil Maclean, observed James and noted that his description matched that of the man wanted in England for a post office robbery. They approached and questioned him. James was not able to provide a satisfactory account of his movements and was arrested under suspicion of robbery. MacDonald, who was standing in The Parade waiting, observed the whole incident. Unseen by the police, he melted away into the crowd.

Meanwhile, at the police station, a body search of James revealed £1,250 secreted about his person and he was charged with robbery. Detectives from Mansfield travelled to Fort William and returned James to England to face trial. John MacDonald must have spent many a sleepless night, expecting a sharp knock on the door from police officers. But surprisingly, and to his great relief, it did not come. Joseph James confessed to the theft in its entirety, claiming he had acted alone. The police had no reason to suspect otherwise, since James was in possession of nearly all the takings from the robbery at the time of his arrest. James pled guilty and served eighteen months in prison. His defence in court being that, in a moment of madness, the sight of that large a sum of money had affected his mind.

After the weeks passed, with Joseph James in prison and the case now closed, John MacDonald became more confident again. He still believed that levels of security within the post office network were substantially poorer than those in place at Britain's banks. He now realised that using a post office employee was too obvious a ploy. Although he did plan to repay Joseph James' loyalty at a later stage, for his next robbery he intended to act alone.

After a visit to Fort William Post Office in the High Street in September 1929, posing as a customer, he was able to clearly see the sorting office to the rear of customer counters, through an open door. The post office was busy and in the days prior to CCTV cameras there was little chance in anyone remembering him. Then, following a night-time recce of the premises, he was able to ascertain that by using the dimly lit MacRae's Lane to the side of the post office, he would be unobserved at night in the shadows to the rear of the building. Assuring that his planned robbery was synchronised with the railway company's timetable, he allowed himself one hour to break into the premises, open the smaller (and less heavily secured) safe, exit the building and casually walk along the High Street, wearing his overalls and carrying his toolbag, through Station Square and board the night train to begin his shift. By morning, and the discovery of the theft, he would safely be in London.

When the post office clerks arrived to open the premises at 8.45am the following morning, they discovered that the rear door to the building had been levered from its hinges and the sorting room door opened. Once inside, the unknown thief or thieves had targeted only the smaller of the safes. Using what seemed like a minimum of effort the door to the safe had been removed and a number of registered packets and some banknotes removed. The combined value of the theft was estimated at £400 (approximately £25,000 today). Once again, the larger safes were untouched. Despite a thorough investigation by the police and the Post Office Detective Department no clues were forthcoming, and the case file for the robbery was eventually closed.

The robbery of Fort William Post Office was not to be a solitary affair, however. A repeat of the offence occurred in February 1930, again in July of the same year, and once more in December. On the final occasion the thief, under cover of darkness, had climbed onto the flat roof at the rear of the building, smashed the rooflight, and then dropped down directly onto the floor of the sorting room, probably using a rope. Again, the safe had been expertly opened, without causing any apparent damage, leaving the police to conclude that the perpetrators had access to a set of keys. Yet again, a number of registered packets had been removed. The thief had then stacked a pile of furniture to enable him to climb back out through the broken rooflight, without disturbing any of the nearby tenants. Perhaps John MacDonald, flushed with cash, had been able to bribe a member of the Post Office staff into copying a set of keys for him?

No suspicion ever fell on MacDonald, who was able to continue his routine unencumbered. His certainty in his carefully thought through cover story seems to have been justified. A workman casually walking to the railway station, carrying his toolbag, does not appear to have raised the suspicions of the police or public. Indeed, he was even questioned by the police as a witness when he was recognised by a member of the public walking through the double arched entrance into the railway station, following one of the burglaries. Asked if he seen anything or anyone unusual while walking to work, he coolly replied that he had not. He then casually turned around, carrying his LMS toolbag (which, of course, doubled as his burglary kit) and boarded the locomotive.

The December 1930 robbery, like those previously, remained unsolved, and MacDonald continued to be employed by the LMS railway, travelling the length and breadth of Britain's railway network without arousing suspicion, spending his weeknights at lodgings in London, enjoying the bright lights of the metropolis, before returning to his wife and children on the Isle of Skye at weekends.

During the next two years, a staggering number of unsolved post office raids were perpetrated across the country, including robberies in Glasgow, Edinburgh, London, the Midlands, and again in Fort William. Many of these offences were in close proximity to a railway station on the LMS network, and it seems highly likely MacDonald was involved in many of these.

However, the good looking, intelligent, and increasingly confident John MacDonald had other, far grander plans. His personal life and his career path, utilising some of the ill-gotten gains from his series of post office robberies, was about to take an unexpected and surprising twist. But not before his next planned post office break-in almost ended tragically for one terrified post office employee.

THE GREAT TRAIN ROBBERY

By the mid-1930s John MacDonald – still only in his mid-twenties - had every right to feel rather pleased with himself, perhaps even a little smug. He had been given the nickname 'Ramsay' (after the leader of the Labour Party), which he rather relished. His friend Joseph James had now been released from prison, meaning there was now no risk that James would trade MacDonald's name for a reduced prison sentence.

MacDonald himself had never been questioned regarding any of the spate of Post Office robberies that had taken place in towns along the LMS railways network. With a sizeable amount of cash secreted away, he was able to keep his wife and children in Portree on the Isle of Skye well catered for, and, in addition, rent a large apartment in Clarendon Street, a desirable road of sought-after Georgian villas in Pimlico, south west London. As he spent his weeknights in the capital city, MacDonald had taken a mistress, a girl named Jean Hamilton-Smith, who took great pleasure in spending the money that MacDonald had 'earned.' He enjoyed showing Jean off to his friends, savouring the excitement of his secret double life. Nevertheless, to compensate for MacDonald's long unexplained absences, Jean required large amounts of money 'to keep her sweet', as MacDonald explained to his friends. He duly obliged, quickly whittling away the proceeds from his criminal activities in the process. Jean, naturally, had no knowledge of MacDonald's wife on the Isle of Skye. In turn, his wife was blissfully unaware of Jean Hamilton-Smith's existence.

MacDonald, with his thirst for thrills and yet more money was not contented with his run of good fortune so far. His good looks and easy-going charm attracted attention wherever he went and a throwaway comment made to him in a public house one evening was to ultimately lead to his demise.

During a weekend on Skye, MacDonald had been drinking in the bar at the Portree Hotel, boasting to anyone who would listen about the ease with which he had attracted women, while travelling on the railway networks. One of the onlookers sarcastically remarked, 'I don't know why you don't become a film star, Ramsay?' MacDonald, instead of brushing off the humorous remark, decided that it was something he was entirely capable of doing.

On his return to London, he paid a large amount of money for a photographic portfolio, then paid 'introduction' fees to several London theatrical agencies, in order that his name might be put forward for film roles. MacDonald's résumé described him as '6ft tall, strong, with fair hair and blue eyes' (although he may have used a little

artistic licence - his passport records his height as 5'10"!).
MacDonald enrolled for acting lessons and, with the help
of Jean, invested in several new suits of clothes. He was
rewarded with small, non-speaking, roles in *Red Ensign,*
released in 1934, *The 39 Steps* in 1935, *The Captain's Table* in
1936, and *Kidnapped* in 1938, among others. So confident
was MacDonald that fame would surely follow that he
walked away from his job with the LMS, determined to
become a full-time actor. Sadly, for John MacDonald, it was
not to be.

By the middle of 1937 he had worked his way through
almost all the money he had stolen. With rent due on his
Pimlico flat and hungry mouths to feed on Skye he decided
to return to his old ways.

When returning to Skye one day in January 1938, during
an overnight stop in Glasgow, he decided to attempt
another post office heist, this time with a prop gun he had
stolen from a film set at Shepperton Studies. MacDonald
walked into a small post office and stationers on the Old
Govan Road, just as the shop was about to close at 7pm. He
entered the public telephone call-box in the corner, as if to
make a telephone call, and waited for the other customers
to leave. As soon as the shop was empty, he approached the
assistant demanded access to the safe, 'pardon me miss,
it's money I want'. When she bravely refused, MacDonald
was forced to strike her across the temple using the butt
of the fake revolver. In a panic, he bound her to a chair,
struck her again, and threatened her until she gave up
the location of the keys. He rifled the safe, removing
whatever cash he could. However, as he did so, a woman

passing by on the street outside overheard the young shop assistant's scream. She quickly ran to fetch help, which fortuitously gave MacDonald just enough time to escape into the gloom of the night. It had been a narrow escape for the thief, who spent an uneasy night waiting for the next train to Fort William and safety. The uncharacteristic change in behaviour may have come from financial desperation. Nevertheless, it now meant that the police had a description of the man they wanted to question. In desperation, MacDonald decided to give up his aspirations of stardom, and keep a much lower profile.

He re-applied for a fitter's job at the railway station office in Fort William, and from there returned to the safety of London, where he felt he had placed sufficient distance between himself and the Glasgow City Police.

Meanwhile, he continued to spend his weekends on the Isle of Skye and his weeknights in London with his mistress. However, with the proceeds of the Glasgow robbery being quickly frittered away, how much longer would he be able to sustain his expensive lifestyle without, once again, resorting to crime?

The answer to that question came in May of 1938. MacDonald had found the long hours and hard graft as a fitter no longer to his taste; and instead taken employment with the London Passenger Transport Board (LPTB) as a mechanic on the London Underground network. It was while working at Earls Court Tube station that he noticed an opportunity that might mean he would never need to work again. It seemed too good to be true. MacDonald noticed that on Thursday afternoons a large amount of cash was routinely carried from the branch of Lloyd's Bank on the corner of Earls Court Road and Hogarth Place, through the entrance to the Underground station on the opposite side of the road. The money was then taken through an interior door (accessible to only LPTB employees), along a narrow passageway and onto the waiting underground carriages from where the money was then distributed as weekly wage packets for staff working at the various stations along the District and Piccadilly Lines. During his shifts MacDonald closely observed the transit of the money. The cash was always carried in two metal strongboxes from the bank, across the busy Earls Court Road by the bank's security guards. To attempt to steal the money at this point would be too risky, in full view of the large number of pedestrians, buses and motor cars on Earls Court Road, and in broad daylight too.

At the entrance to the station, the strongboxes were transferred from the security guards into the custody of two LPTB employees. Clearly, once on the Underground train, and in a confined space, it would be enormously problematic to execute a robbery, let alone make an easy escape. The narrow external passageway, although it was bordered by a fence constructed of 6-foot-high iron railings, appeared to offer the best potential site for the heist, providing the gang could steal the cashboxes before they reached the safety of the District Line platform. Nevertheless, MacDonald knew that the heist would need to be planned down to the finest detail, and it was not a job he could undertake alone.

Whilst working in the signal office at the station, he had noticed that the two porters entrusted to carry the strongboxes inside the station complex were not large, and neither did they appear to be particularly strong or intimidating. With the right team in place, MacDonald knew that he would be able to snatch the strongboxes without too much resistance. His appetite for the theft was increased tenfold when he overheard the porters mentioning that the boxes contained the wages of up to 300 men.

MacDonald began his planning for the robbery by meeting two associates, John Dalling and Harold Wardrope, at the Earls Court Tavern. MacDonald explained his plan, emphasising how simple he believed the robbery would be; and hoping that Dalling could supply a getaway car. However, the two men were not interested, and MacDonald instead decided to recruit his old colleagues from the Scots Guards, Alexander MacRae, John Cook, and Joseph James. MacRae and Cook, who were both working in London at the time, agreed to take part. James, however, declined. MacDonald explained his plan and the date for the robbery was fixed for Thursday 19th May 1938.

Firstly, MacDonald terminated his lease for the flat in Clarendon Street and rented a 'safe house' for himself and Jean in the less salubrious surroundings of Buckingham Gate in Victoria. At 1pm in the afternoon of 19th May, MacDonald and MacRae placed themselves in a window seat at The Prince of Teck public house, on the corner of Kenway Road and Earls Court Road, less than a hundred yards from the entrance to the Underground station. From this vantage point the two men could clearly observe John Cook, who had taken up position on the opposite side of Earls Court Road, on its junction with Trebovir Road, from where he could clearly see both the entrance to Lloyd's Bank and the public house. Cook, as instructed, leant casually against a lamppost reading a newspaper. MacDonald had reasoned that it might appear too suspicious if the three men were seen loitering together outside the station, with too many potential witnesses on the pavement or in the surrounding buildings.

At approximately 2pm Cook observed the security staff from Lloyd's Bank open the bank's front door, carrying two metal strongboxes. Cook carefully watched as the guards waited for a gap in the traffic and began to cross the road towards the underground station. He promptly folded his newspaper, in a pre-arranged signal, and started walking quickly down Trebovir Road to the side of the station. MacDonald and MacRae hurriedly jostled past the other customers and left The Prince of Teck. Turning left, they made their way quickly along Earls Court Road towards the tiled and brick arched station entrance. MacDonald had calculated that he would have less than five minutes to complete the heist, from the time the strongboxes had left the bank, the handover procedure had been completed in the station concourse, and the two LPTB employees entrusted to carry the money would be safely behind the locked door, which in turn led them along the external passageway towards the safety of the busy District Line platform and a secure carriage.

MacDonald and MacRae, dressed in LPTB overalls, with flat caps and wearing gloves and false spectacles, walked straight past the two employees charged with carrying the strongboxes, and made their way, completely unnoticed among the hubbub of the busy station, behind the door marked 'Private - LPTB Staff Only', and into the shadowy passageway. They secreted themselves as best they could, 50 yards along the passageway, among the shadows, and watched carefully as the two porters, Harold Thomas and John Schofield, entered the passageway through the door from the concourse. The two porters paid little attention to what lay ahead of them in the passageway, assuming that their brief journey to the District Line platform would be as uneventful as usual. Instead, they concentrated on locking the door behind themselves and in carrying the heavy boxes. Suddenly, as they approached the point where the two thieves crouched half hidden, there was a flurry of commotion as MacDonald and MacRae leapt forward. MacRae pushed Schofield violently, causing him to strike his head against the wall and collapse. He dropped the heavy strongbox, which clattered to the ground. MacDonald pulled a rubber cosh from his overall pockets

and lashed Harold Thomas across the head with one
savage swing of his right arm. The blow knocked Thomas
sideways and he, too, struck the wall, banging his head and
rendering him semi-conscious.

Acting quickly, MacDonald and MacRae removed three
large, folded, heavy-duty mailbags they had concealed
about their person (presumably stolen during one of
MacDonald's previous post office robberies) and carefully
placed the metal cash boxes inside two of the bags. They
then took the third mailbag and laid it over the top of
the iron railings that led to the back of the buildings on
Trebovir Street. With the mailbag in place, it was easy
to manoeuvre themselves and the mailbags containing
the cashboxes over the railings. Once on the other side
and screened from view by the trees in the gardens of
Kensington Mansions, they quickly made their way through
the gardens and onto Trebovir Street, where John Cook
sat waiting, with the engine running, in the gang's getaway
car, an inconspicuous Morris work van. MacDonald and
MacRae climbed into the rear, attempting to appear like
two workmen being picked up after a long shift. Cook then
quickly pulled away, turning left onto Warwick Road as the
three men melted away among the London traffic, before
the alarm had even been raised. The whole operation had
taken less than ten minutes.

Once back at MacDonald's Victoria flat, the men changed
clothes and hid the metal boxes under the bed. Jean asked
MacDonald who the two other men were, telling him
that she felt ill and did not want anyone else in the flat.
MacDonald instructed her to, 'Go to bed, we have to go out
again, we'll be back later'.

He only referred to the two other men as 'M' and 'C', but Jean did overhear him say, 'M You wear my coat, get a taxi and throw the case over Chelsea Bridge. C! You're a fine man to drive the getaway van. You nearly drove us into a lamppost!'

With that, the men left. MacDonald returned at 11pm alone. Thinking Jean was asleep, he lit the fire and proceeded to burn his flat cap, spectacles, and some papers. However, Jean surprised him,

'What are you doing?' she asked.

'Mind your own business and go to sleep. It's nothing to do with you!'

Jean replied, 'Don't shout, I don't feel well, I think I might need to go to the doctor's'.

MacDonald informed her that he needed to leave. He handed her £2 saying, 'This is to for coal and to pay the rent'.

Clearly surprised, Jean inquired, 'Where did you get the money from?'

'I borrowed it', came MacDonald's answer, 'and I could borrow plenty more if I wanted to!'

With that, he left, taking his share of the money with him. The total stolen from Earl's Court totalled £1,141 15s 10d (approximately £80,000 today), around half of the amount MacDonald had hoped would be contained in the boxes.

Within 48 hours MacDonald had travelled by train,

boarded the ferry at Mallaig, and returned to the safety of Portree on Skye. A long way from the scene of the robbery in London, he assumed he was free and clear. MacDonald gave his mother a crisp English white £5 note and told her, 'there's plenty more where that came from!'

However, it was not to be a happy ending for John MacDonald. Scotland Yard in London launched an immediate investigation into the heist. The mailbag, carelessly left draped over the iron railings behind Earl's Court station, was taken away to be examined. In addition, a reward was offered for information leading to an arrest. Unfortunately for John MacDonald, the two men he had first asked to assist him in the robbery, John Dalling and Harold Wardrope, were only too happy to inform the police that they had been approached earlier in the year by MacDonald. After discovering that MacDonald had been employed at Earl's Court station and had not been seen since the day of the robbery, the police were soon on his trail.

After another tip off they raided his flat in Buckingham Gate, at which they found a less than happy Jean Hamilton-Smith. Presumably rather annoyed to discover that her partner had a wife and family on the Isle of Skye, Jean identified the mailbag used in the robbery as one she had seen before and also gave the police a full statement detailing MacDonald's movements on the 19th May. The investigating officers also found remnants of the disguises worn by the thieves among the ashes in the fireplace. Armed with this evidence, it did not take them long to track down John MacDonald.

Greatly to MacDonald's surprise, Detective-Sergeant George Williams and Detective Carter knocked on the door of MacDonald's cottage in Portree on 24th May. Dumbfounded, he was arrested and taken to the Kyle of Lochalsh Police Station on the mainland, where he was charged with robbery. In response he answered, 'Thanks very much. I am not saying anything, and I have already had that explained to me.'

When questioned about the origin of the £5 banknote he had given to his mother, MacDonald responded: 'I did not know she had one, and if you think that it is any of the money from Earl's Court you are unlucky. Anyhow, there is other money you should be concerning yourself with besides mine. I am lucky at racing. I am not going to tell you where the note came from, and if I did give it to my mother that is my business!'

Eventually, however, under the weight of evidence and questioning, MacDonald crumbled. He explained to Sergeant Williams that he, 'had two brothers who were a little bit mental; and sometimes I go like that myself. I might have been like that at Earl's Court, although I do not remember. I think I should see a doctor. I may need to be put in a mental home instead of being sent to prison.'

Ultimately, it may have been a ploy by MacDonald to lessen his sentence. He also turned 'King's evidence', giving the Scottish police the names and locations of his co-conspirators in the robbery. In addition, MacDonald also admitted to a string of further offences stretching back over almost a decade.

As he was transported by train from Fort William to London for sentencing, MacDonald glanced for the last time at the beautiful lochs and mountains of Lochaber. He turned to Sergeant Williams and remarked, 'I wonder if I will see such scenery as that again? Still, I suppose London and its women have been my ruin.'

In July 1938 he was sentenced to 4 years imprisonment, with hard labour – a sentence considered by many to be far too lenient.

Following his release in 1942 he returned to Scotland a changed man. After the Second World War he emigrated to Canada, via a roundabout route through the United States, eventually entering Canada via the St Alban's Border Crossing in Vermont. This circuitous route may have been necessary as his criminal record would certainly have precluded him from entering Canada directly from Scotland.

John MacDonald died alone in Canada in 1957 at the young age of 48.

THE FLANNAN ISLES LIGHTHOUSE MYSTERY

On Saturday 15th December 1900 the steamship *Archer* was en route from Philadelphia to Edinburgh. Severe storms had battered the whole of Britain for most of the month, even knocking over one of the lintels and huge stones at Stonehenge! Conditions in the north Atlantic were atrocious too. As the *Archer* battled its way around the Flannan Isles, 15 miles to the west of Lewis and Harris, on its journey to the east coast of Scotland, the crew were surprised to see that the light from the Flannan Isles Lighthouse was not working. In such poor visibility the recently commissioned lighthouse should have been operational. The anomaly was noted in the ship's log. However, in the days before ship-to-shore radio communication, the discrepancy could not be reported until the *Archer* docked.

Once the vessel was safely moored in Leith Harbour three days later, the captain reported the incident to the Northern Lighthouse Board (the organisation responsible for marine navigation around the Scottish coastline). It also transpired that crofters inhabiting the shorelands of

western Lewis had reported that they had not observed
the light for several nights. Initially this did not surprise the
crofters, as a thick sea-fog had obscured the light on several
previous occasions. However, when the fog cleared, and no
light was visible, the authorities became apprehensive. It
was decided that the matter required urgent investigation,
and with no direct communication possible with the island,
a relief vessel, the lighthouse tender *Hesperus*, was ordered
to make its way to the lighthouse. Unfortunately, due to
the continuing adverse weather conditions, the *Hesperus*
was unable to sail from Breasclete, in Lewis, as planned,
on 20th December. It would eventually reach the Flannan
Isles around noon on Wednesday 26th December, only to be
greeted by a perplexing mystery.

Of the seven uninhabited islands that make up the
archipelago known as the Flannan Islands, Eilean Mòr is
the largest and the highest. Although an ideal location
for the placing of the newly planned lighthouse in 1895,
construction could not have been more difficult and would
take four long years. The islands offered the Northern
Lighthouse Board's construction crews no point at which
a landing could be easily affected without incurring great
difficulty or danger. With no natural beaches or shoreline,
amongst some of the stormiest seas in the world, and north
Atlantic swells that only permit safe landings at the height
of summer, landing-stages were hewn from the rock using
dynamite. All of the materials used needed to be hauled
up the 200-foot cliffs by wire pulleys, directly from supply
boats, no trivial task in the face of the turbulent Atlantic
tides and gales. A shore station at Breasclete on the Isle of

Lewis was also added. The oil-fired lamps on the Flannan
Islands Lighthouse – visible for many miles - were first lit on
7th December 1899, sending a most welcome warning signal
out across the hostile waters of the Atlantic.

The relief vessel *Hesperus* finally arrived at the rock on
Boxing Day 1900 carrying a relief lighthouse man Joseph
Moore, from the shore station on Lewis. As the *Hesperus*
hove to off the east landing stage, James Harvey, the
captain, blew the ship's whistle and sent up a flare – the
usual signal when approaching; enabling the lighthouse
keepers enough time to make final preparations for the

safe mooring of any incoming vessel and the handing
ashore of mail and stores, etc. However, no return signal
was received, nor was the flag raised on the island's
flagpole. Captain Harvey thought the situation was
unusual, as he knew that three men should have been
on duty at the time (James Ducat, Thomas Marshall, and
Donald MacArthur).

When the *Hesperus* reached her anchorage point, it became
obvious that the east landing point displayed no evidence
that the keepers were even expecting a relief vessel.
(Occasionally it was possible for ships to arrive at the west
landing stage, on the other side of island, however this was
checked and also found to be empty). Eventually Joseph
Moore, the relief keeper, was dropped ashore by small boat.
Ordinarily, he would have been greeted on the landing
stage by the lightkeeper whom it was intended for him to
replace.

While the relief ship rode at anchor at a safe distance from
Eilean Mòr, far enough away to avoid being dashed against
the cliffs in the event of a sudden change in the wind's
direction, Joseph Moore hastened up the long flights of
rocky steps to the lighthouse. He found the small gate to
the enclosure shut. The two outer doors were also closed.
Moore flung them open with a loud clang, but there was
still no sign of movement inside. He decided to investigate
and immediately headed for the living area. This was
also unoccupied and eerily quiet. In the fireplace lay the
cold, dead cinders of the last fire the missing lightkeepers
had enjoyed. The fire provided some welcome warmth on a

cold winter's day, yet it had seemingly been left to die out.
On the mantelpiece stood the lighthouse clock, stopped
and unmoving. Its wind-up mechanism had been allowed
to run itself down to a standstill. It occurred to Moore that,
perhaps, his companions had overslept. He called out; but
received no answer, his voice echoing around the confines
of the building. Next, he hurried into the bedroom but
it too was empty. The beds had been used, and clothes
hung in the lockers, but the room was empty.

Worried and perplexed, he returned to the East Landing
stage to summon help from the ship. Two of the ship's
crew were put ashore with difficulty, as the seas were still
rough, and the three men immediately set about making a
thorough search of the island. The three men searched all
of the lighthouse buildings, the islands, cliffs and landing
stages. Everything appeared to be in perfect order. There
was no sign of any trouble, or disturbance, nor was anything
missing or seemingly out of place. The derricks and cranes
on the landing stages were just as they had been left on
the previous relief journey a few weeks earlier. Even the
jib was still secured to the rocks below and the tarpaulin
remained intact around the barrel of the crane, where it
had been secured to protect it from the sea spray. In fact,
the only thing that appeared out of place was the discovery
that a storage box, normally kept in a hollow in the rocks,
and containing spare ropes and handles for the crane,
appeared to have been carried away in a storm. Several of
the ropes from the storage box were found strewn along
the face of the cliffs nearby. Yet no effort had been made
to retrieve them. The twisted iron hand railings on the

lower stone staircase showed that the west landing had also
been subjected to the effects of a violent storm. In addition,
it appeared that a huge boulder weighing at least a ton had
been displaced by the violence of the tempest. Although
the landing stages showed definite evidence of damage
caused by the huge swells, this did not explain the complete
disappearance of the three men.

An idea suddenly suggested itself to Joseph Moore. He
ran back and checked the keepers' living quarters again.
Neither James Ducat's nor Thomas Marshall's sea-boots
and oilskins were to be found. Joseph Moore, who knew the
routine of both the lighthouse and his companions well,
knew that only when setting out to inspect the landing-
stages in stormy conditions did the men put on their boots
and oilskins. The third keeper's boots and oilskin were
still stored in their proper place, however. This seemed to
indicate that he may have left the safety of the lighthouse
in a hurry. The only explanation Joseph Moore and the
Hesperus captain James Harvey could arrive at, was that
the men, anxious to ensure that everything was doubly
secure at the west landing stage during a severe storm, had
been swept away by a huge wave crashing into the cliffs.

Joseph Moore and three volunteers from the ship were left
on the island to man the lighthouse, while Captain Harvey
returned to Lewis with the ship. Once there, he sent an
urgent telegram to the Northern Lighthouse Board:

26 Dec 1900,

*A dreadful accident has happened at the Flannans. The three
keepers, Ducat, Marshall and the Occasional have disappeared
from the Island. The clocks were stopped and other signs indicated
that the accident must have happened about a week ago. Poor
fellows they must have been blown over the cliffs or drowned trying
to secure a crane.*
Captain J Harvey, Hesperus

Captain Harvey's telegram was far from favourably
received by the Northern Lighthouse Board. It was
thought to be extremely unlikely that three experienced
lightkeepers would all risk their own lives simultaneously
at the perilous west landing in such appalling weather.
Nevertheless, the thorough search of the island had
revealed nothing. No bodies or clues were ever found, apart
from the diary entries made by James Ducat, the principal
keeper, in the Lighthouse Log:

*Wed 12th Dec. 1900 - 'severe winds have been blowing from the
west, the likes of which I have never seen before in twenty years'*
*Thu 13th Dec. 1900 - 'the gale continues. Thomas Marshall has
been very quiet and Donald MacArthur has been crying'*
Fri 14th Dec. 1900 - 'the storm is still raging; we are all praying'
*Sat 15th Dec. 1900 - '9am. Storm is ended, sea calm. God is over
all'*

An inquiry was immediately ordered and Superintendent
Robert Muirhead, from the Northern Lighthouse Board,
was despatched to the island to conduct the official

investigation into the incident. Muirhead had originally recruited all three of the missing men and knew them personally.

He examined the clothing left behind in the lighthouse and concluded that James Ducat and Thomas Marshall had gone down to the west landing stage at the height of the storm, and that Donald McArthur (known as the 'Occasional' keeper) had left the lighthouse during heavy rain in his shirt sleeves, perhaps to see why his colleagues had not returned, perhaps to warn them of an incoming wave he had observed from the lighthouse. Robert Muirhead noted that whoever had left the lighthouse last, 'had left it unattended in breach of NLB rules'. He also noted that the damage to 'the west landing was difficult to believe unless actually seen'.

Ducat's final entry in the log was dated Saturday, 15th December and was timed at 9am How soon afterwards the tragedy followed, no one can say precisely; however' there are several important clues. It may well have been later in the morning of that same day, or perhaps at some point in the early afternoon. Following the final log entry at 9am the routine duties had been performed. For instance, the big lamps in the lantern-tower had been trimmed in readiness for another spell of service. The oil fountains and canteens were all primed. The lenses and mechanism of the lamp had been cleaned according to the daily routine. These undertakings were all known to require a certain amount of time; and had definitely been attended to after 9am on that morning. The relief lighthouse keeper,

Joseph Moore, also reported that, 'The kitchen utensils were all very clean, which is a sign that it must be after dinner some time they left.' Finally (as mentioned at the beginning of this story), the captain of the steamship *Archer* had reported that, by midnight on December 15th, he was unable to see the Flannan Light.

Therefore, Robert Muirhead was able to conclude:

We can fix fairly accurately the day on which this haunting tragedy occurred, and perhaps also, within reasonable limits, the hour of that day. From evidence which I was able to procure I was satisfied that the men had been on duty up till dinner time on Saturday the 15th of December, that they had gone down to secure a box in which the mooring ropes, landing ropes etc. were kept, and which was secured in a crevice in the rock about 110 ft above sea level, and that an extra-large sea had rushed up the face of the rock, had gone above them, and coming down with immense force, had swept them completely away.

Whether this explanation brought any comfort to the families of the lost keepers (Ducat left a wife and four children; MacArthur a wife and two children) is unknown.

What really happened may never be known; however, a number of theories and counter-theories, cultural references and bizarre explanations have been proposed over the years that followed.

The alluring and long-lasting mystery has led to much conjecture since 1900. Almost immediately after the

tragedy, newspapers and periodicals began to speculate
wildly. Implausible stories were published including the
story of a huge sea serpent, or giant seabird, that had
carried the men away, or the rumour that the three keepers
had arranged for a ship to carry them away to start new lives
abroad. Many thought they had been abducted by foreign
spies; or they had met their fate through the malevolent
presence of a ghost, perhaps the 'Phantom of the Seven
Hunters' (a popular Hebridean legend).

In more modern times other explanations and theories
have been presented. Subsequent lighthouse keepers on
Eilean Mòr have reported seeing huge waves approaching
the narrow gullies and caves on the west side of the island.
These waves explode against the rocks with such force they
are easily capable of washing a man out to sea. Perhaps
Donald MacArthur may have seen a series of large waves
approaching the island and, knowing the likely danger to
his colleagues, ran down to the landing stage to warn them,
only to be washed away himself in the violent swell?

Recent research by author James Love discovered that
Thomas Marshall had previously been docked five shillings
from his wages, for 'failing to secure his equipment'
during a huge gale. It is likely, in seeking to avoid another
penalty, that he and James Ducat had tried to secure their
equipment during a storm and were swept away as a result.
James Love speculates that MacArthur probably, and rather
hurriedly, had tried to warn or help his colleagues and was
also swept out to sea. This theory may also explain why
MacArthur's set of oilskins remained hanging on their peg,

while Ducat and Marshall's were gone.

Further speculation points to the psychology of the keepers. Allegedly Donald MacArthur was a volatile and violent character; this may have led to a fight breaking out near the cliff edge, close to the West Landing, causing all three men to plunge to their deaths. Another theory claims that one of the men went insane, murdered the other two, then threw their bodies into the sea, before jumping in himself in a fit of remorse.

Whatever the reason, four questions remain unanswered. Firstly, why were no bodies ever found? Accidents and shipwrecks were extremely common during the 19th century and the majority of victim's bodies would invariably wash ashore somewhere on the Scottish islands or west coast, taken there by the unforgiving winds and tides. Secondly, why were the two doors to the lighthouse and the gate all closed? If Donald MacArthur did rush outside to the aid of his comrades, is it plausible to assume that he did not have time to put on his oilskins, yet did have time to carefully close the doors and gate behind him? Thirdly, knowing, as they undoubtedly did, the perils of an Atlantic storm and sea swell, why would three experienced lighthouse keepers leave the safety of a secure building 150 feet above the crashing breakers, and venture down to the most dangerous point on the island?

Finally, and perhaps, most strangely of all, on the 12th, 13th and 14th December (when James Ducat had recorded horrendous storms in the lighthouse logbook), no other passing ship, nor any of the islanders on nearby Lewis and

Harris, reported any gales or storms.

The story of the Flannan Islands Lighthouse mystery
has entered popular culture over the past century or so;
with much of the 'evidence' being called into question.
However, the intriguing enigma still puzzles many, even
today. Versions of the events have appeared in two recent
Hollywood films (*The Vanishing* in 2018 and *The Lighthouse*
in 2019), as well as a Doctor Who story, *Horror of Fang Rock*,
and a song by Genesis, *The Mystery of Flannan Isle Lighthouse*.
Subsequent lighthouse keepers on the island, as well as
visitors, have reported hearing ghostly cries from the sea
at night. A suspicious and even supernatural element to
the story has been given great impetus by a poem entitled
Flannan Isle, published in 1912 by Wilfred Wilson Gibson:

> *Yet, as we crowded through the door,*
> *We only saw a table, spread*
> *For dinner, meat and cheese and bread;*
> *But, all untouched; and no one there:*
> *As though, when they sat down to eat,*
> *Ere they could even taste,*
> *Alarm had come; and they in haste*
> *Had risen and left the bread and meat:*
> *For at the table-head a chair*
> *Lay tumbled on the floor.*

THE PRINCE ACROSS THE WATER
(PART ONE)

In *Blood Beneath Ben Nevis,* I laid out the tale of Bonnie Prince Charlie's missing gold and all the known clues to its hidden location. The famous, and long-lost fortune in louis d'or gold coins had arrived from France just too late to aid the Jacobite cause on that fateful, cold, and sleety April morning in 1746 at the Battle of Culloden. But, with the battle lost, the Highlanders in disarray, and the vengeful redcoats in pursuit, what became of the prince himself?

On 30th April, two weeks after the calamity at Culloden (and unaware of the Jacobites' defeat), two French frigates, the *Bellona* and *Mars,* had successfully navigated the Ardnamurchan peninsula and were landing at a remote spot in Loch nan Uamh on Scotland's west coast; bringing with them the legendary lost gold. At that moment, however, the defeated Prince was less than 100 miles away – not on the mainland, but across the Little Minch in the Outer Hebrides - attempting to escape his pursuers. Three days earlier, driven by a violent storm, the boat carrying Prince Charles Stuart had taken refuge at Rossinish on the Isle of Benbecula, between North and South Uist. Once there, his small party remained, sheltering and recovering for two days in a deserted hut. One of the men collected what kindling he could, in the hope of lighting a fire to help dry the prince's clothes. Determined to make for Stornoway, they set sail again under a cloak of darkness on the evening of 29th April. Unknown to the Prince, his small boat had run aground on the storm-swept coast of Scalpay, a small island off the east coast of Lewis, just as the gold coins were being unloaded on the shores of Loch nan Uamh on the mainland. However, this terrifying night-time voyage from Benbecula to Scalpay formed only part of the prince's incredible escape from the terrible clutches of British justice undoubtedly waiting for him at the hands of William Augustus, the Duke of Cumberland.

These two chapters tell the full story of the 'Prince over the water', his retreat from Culloden, and the brave and loyal believers who assisted him.

On the night preceding the battle, Friday 15th April 1746, the fatigued Jacobite forces had trudged their weary way to Culloden across boggy ground. Their attempted night-time raid on the Royal Army's camp at Nairn (where the redcoats were celebrating the Duke of Cumberland's birthday) had been a failure. More bad news was to follow for the exhausted Jacobite troops. An officer with Lochiel's regiment, who had become separated from his own regiment after falling asleep in a wood, warned the Prince of the advancing government troops. However, the caution was not fully heeded, as many of the Jacobite soldiers had already dispersed in search of food, many had been stationed elsewhere, some had returned to Inverness, while others lay asleep, cold, and exhausted, in ditches and outbuildings. In fact, it seems likely that several hundred members of the Jacobite army, who might have fought on that day, may have simply missed the battle altogether.

The British force of 9,000 soldiers heavily outnumbered the 5,000 Jacobite men. In addition, the Jacobite forces were hampered by exhaustion, boggy ground, and terrain that suited the Duke of Cumberland's well-rested army and superior mounted division. All told, the fighting lasted less than one hour, Jacobite casualties were estimated at between 1,500-2,000 men killed or wounded, with many of these occurring in the pursuit that immediately followed the battle. The Duke of Cumberland's official list of prisoners taken included 154 Jacobites and 222 'French' prisoners (men from the 'foreign units' in the French service, fighting alongside the Jacobites).

In stark contrast to the overwhelming Jacobite losses, British government casualties were reported as just 50 dead and 259 wounded.

Following Culloden, a proportion of the fleeing Highlanders journeyed towards Inverness where they encountered the 2nd battalion of Lovat's regiment. It has been suggested by historians that Lovat had shrewdly switched sides and turned upon the retreating Jacobites, an act that may explain his remarkable rise in fortune in the years that followed Culloden.

Many of the Jacobites' Lowland regiments headed south, towards the barracks at Ruthven, while the remaining Highland units fled northwards, towards Inverness and onto Fort Augustus. Surprisingly, despite the defeat, many of the Highland troops remained in good spirits and eager to resume the campaign. In fact, at this juncture, continuing Jacobite resistance remained potentially viable – at least in terms of manpower. One third of the Jacobite army had either missed or slept through Culloden, which, along with the survivors from the battle. meant a potential force of up to 6,000 men lay at Prince Charles Stuart's disposal. However, the 1,500 Jacobite soldiers who assembled at Ruthven Barracks, and those at Fort Augustus, received orders from Prince Charles Stuart to the effect that they should disperse until he could return later with French support. The instructions, which seemed a virtual capitulation, were, in fact, issued prematurely as they were not intended to be distributed until after the prince had made a safe return to France:

Alas, I see with grief, at present I can do little for you on this side of the water, and for the only thing that can now be done is to defend yourselves till the French assist you. If not, to be able to make better terms.

If the defeat at Culloden was too terrible for many Scots to bear, then the repercussions and reprisals that followed were to be even worse. Yet, despite the horrific nature of Cumberland's retaliation against the fleeing Jacobites (and anyone that chose to shelter them), the abiding memories are not those of a humiliating defeat. Instead, we are left with a rich legacy of immense courage against overwhelming numbers, tales of personal loyalty, sacrifice, and devotion, and perhaps the most romantic and enduring escape story in history.

On 17th April 1746, the morning after the Battle of Culloden, the Duke of Cumberland issued a written order to his troops, reminding them that 'the public orders of the rebels yesterday was to give us no quarter'. This alleged brutal instruction by Prince Charles Stuart to his followers was used by Cumberland to justify the actions of British government troops. In the days that followed Culloden it was reported by the British troops that copies of the prince's orders had been found on the bodies of fallen Jacobite soldiers. Indeed, versions of these supposed Jacobite instructions were published in several journals. However, it appears that the Jacobite order was nothing more than a clumsy forgery, cynically designed to justify the British actions. In fact, the wording that demanded 'no quarter' be taken, was neither written nor signed by Lord George Murray (on behalf of the prince); and had actually been maladroitly appended to the bottom half of an unrelated declaration, previously published in 1745.

Contemporary accounts record that the moor at Culloden was systemically searched from 18th-20th April by government troops in the hope of locating the prince's body. All those found alive, but wounded were put to death, or stripped and left to die of exposure.

It soon became obvious to the Duke of Cumberland that Prince Charles Stuart had escaped from the scene of the battle and a reward was quickly offered for his capture. The huge sum offered, £30,000 (approximately £7 million today), was designed to loosen even the most patriotic of tongues.

'Butcher' Cumberland, a nickname he more than justified, rode with his troops to Inverness. Men were murdered, for the crime of wearing Highland dress, women were raped and killed, and children slaughtered. Jacobite prisoners were systematically hanged in the streets of the city. One witness reported seeing a blind beggar woman being whipped in the city for not knowing where the prince was hiding. The outlying districts did not escape their share of reprisals either. Entire crofting families were put to death for not revealing the prince's location (of which, of course, they likely had no knowledge).

Cumberland emptied Inverness Jail of British sympathisers, who been imprisoned there by Prince Charles's supporters, instead replacing them with captured Jacobite soldiers. At Cumberland's command, 157 of these Jacobite prisoners were then sent by ship to London to face trial. The conditions on board were so appalling that only 49 men survived the voyage to Tilbury Docks. Those that were fortunate enough to survive reported inhuman treatment on board the vessel, including being whipped for speaking in Gaelic. The higher-ranking Jacobite rebels were executed on Tower Hill in London, whilst the majority of those remaining were sentenced to penal transportation to the British colonies for life, under the terms of the newly enacted *Traitors Transported Act 1746*.

In all, a total of 3,471 Jacobites were captured. Of these, 120 were executed (mostly by hanging, drawing and quartering), more than six hundred died in prison; 936 were transported to the West Indies to be sold as slaves, 121 were banished to remain 'outside our Dominions'. The remaining 1,287 were released or exchanged for other prisoners. Although the true number of Jacobite followers executed by the British will never be known, some estimates put the number as high as 10,000.

Next, to further subjugate the will of the Highlanders, the British Government passed *The Act of Proscription* in 1746, which banned anyone living north of the Highland line from the carrying of arms or the wearing of any Highland dress, especially the kilt, the playing of bagpipes, or the utterance of Gaelic in public. Any transgression was punished with a six-month prison sentence. A second offence resulted in transportation to the colonies. Such was the severity of the legislation and its enactment; the *Act* would have a profound effect on Highland life. Within a few years, the repression of Gaelic culture was almost total.

Despite the heavy bounty of his head, and the intense and terrifying efforts of Cumberland's troops, Prince Charles Stuart somehow managed to remain at large, mostly thanks to the support of his loyal followers.

Travelling with the prince were his two faithful Irish officers, Felix O'Neil, and John O'Sullivan, men whose lack of local knowledge was more than matched by their fierce loyalty. Also accompanying the prince were Lord Elcho, Sir Thomas Sheridan, Alexander MacLeod, Peter MacDermit, and their guide Edward 'Ned' Burke. Immediately following the defeat at Culloden, and as the destiny of the battle became clear, Prince Charles Stuart and his entourage escaped on horseback, travelling via Tordarroch, Aberarder, and Gortleg, and onwards to Fort Augustus. Early on the morning of 17th April he arrived at Invergarry Castle and rested there until around 3pm in the afternoon. The prince, John O'Sullivan, a priest (Allan MacDonald), and Ned Burke, then rode on via Loch Arkaig to Glenpean, and, once there, rested for the night at the home of Donald Cameron, close to the River Pean.

The prince remained at Glenpean awaiting intelligence until 5pm on 18th April, after which, as darkness fell in the valley, he started on foot across the hills for Glen Morar. In the early hours of the following morning, the prince's small party arrived in the braes of Morar, utterly exhausted. Here he was entertained by Angus MacEachine in 'a small sheal house near a wood'.

Following a night walk to Borradale by Glenbeasdale, the prince met Donald MacLeod, tenant of Gualtergill at Borradale, who had been sent as a guide by Æneas MacDonald, Macdonald of Kinlochmoidart's brother (whose home the prince had first stayed in on his landing in Arisaig in 1745). The prince expressed a wish to travel to Sir Alexander MacDonald, or MacLeod of MacLeod, for protection, but Donald thought the prince's plan too dangerous, and arranged instead to guide him across the water to the Hebrides, in the hopes of, once there, obtaining a ship to aid his escape to France. Or, failing that, perhaps even a passage to Orkney or Norway. The prince remained at Borradale while Donald MacLeod attempted to procure a boat and a crew for the hazardous voyage to the Hebrides, without raising suspicion. Whilst waiting, the prince wrote a formal farewell letter to the Clan chiefs who had supported him.

As darkness fell on the night of 26th April 1746, the prince set sail from Lochnanuagh, in a stout eight-oared boat accompanied by O'Sullivan, O'Neil, Allan MacDonald, Donald MacLeod, and Edward Burke, and by eight boatmen. Donald MacLeod had earlier warned the prince not to travel, as a storm was clearly brewing. Charles insisted, however, and his courageous crew battled against the ferocious tempest until they eventually made land, battered and exhausted, at Rossinish on the isolated eastern shores of Benbecula. Here they remained for two days, in a deserted hut (shooting a cow to feed themselves), while they recouped their strength. Legend tells us that the prince promised to recompense the owner of the cow as soon as he was able.

Once the men had recovered from their voyage, the beleaguered party travelled to the house of Mrs McKenzie at the hamlet of Kildun, a few miles from Stornaway. The prince was determined to push on to Stornoway and, once there, hire a boat for Norway. However, the inhabitants of Stornoway, on hearing who the mysterious visitor was, refused to allow the prince to enter the town or hire a vessel. Nevertheless, despite the extreme poverty prevalent in the district, they did not turn the prince over to the British authorities in exchange for the £30,000 reward.

The prince had hoped it might be possible to return to the mainland instead of making for Norway, but Royal Navy ships encircled the islands, frequently landing raiding parties, as the British authorities became convinced of the prince's presence on the long island.

For the next few weeks, the prince and his loyal party dodged the Royal Navy and the local militia, sometimes escaping by boat, with the enemy a matter of a few hundred yards away. On one occasion, shots were fired at them as they made their escape. The prince and his followers took refuge in huts and on remote parts of the islands; occasionally their boat was dashed to the shore by raging storms and violent waves. Cold, wet, and weary they took sanctuary wherever they could. Despite as many as one hundred people on the island being aware of the prince's presence there, he was not betrayed by a single person, even though the huge reward on offer might have been expected to loosen even the most reticent of tongues.

On 15th June the party sailed for the village of Lochboisdale (Gaelic: *Loch Baghasdail*) on South Uist, in the expectation of obtaining some assistance from MacDonald of Boisdale, only to discover that he had already been captured by the British. Seeing several ships on the water blocking their entrance to the harbour, and soldiers patrolling the shore close by, they concealed themselves until nightfall, when they entered Lochboisdale and took shelter in an old, unused tower on a promontory close to the shore. Here they remained for a few days, sometimes sailing up and down the loch to avoid the land-based search parties, or sleeping in open fields at night, using the sails from their boat as shelter against the wind and rain.

Veiled by darkness on the night of Tuesday 21st June, the prince's party crossed the mountains arriving at a hut, near Ormacleit Castle, at midnight. It was here that Charles first met Flora MacDonald (then aged only 24); and asked her assistance in conveying him to the Isle of Skye. Although at first reluctant to help as her stepfather was an officer in the local militia, Flora eventually agreed to do so, her loyalty to the House of Stuart and the Macdonalds of Clanranald forcing her hand. An ingenious scheme was hatched to smuggle the prince away from the islands and out of the country. Unfortunately, a clampdown by the redcoat soldiers required anyone wishing to leave the island by boat to obtain a written permit first. Flora, fortunately for the prince, managed to obtain one via her stepfather.

On the evening of Tuesday 28th June, as darkness was falling, the prince, cunningly disguised as Flora's female Irish maid Betty Burke, was joined by Flora MacDonald, her cousin Neil MacEachen, and four boatmen, as they slipped away to make their escape across the treacherous and inky black waters that led to Skye. The incident would become one of the most celebrated and romantic moments in Scottish history, the triumph of courage and ingenuity against a larger enemy, with profound recriminations for all those involved. Flora MacDonald would become immortalized in folklore, and the tale of the prince's dash for freedom would be recorded in literature, story, and song, *The Syke Boat Song* (below) perhaps being the most enduring example.

The events of that fateful night seem so unlikely as to be little more than an embellished folk tale. Fortunately, however, we still have a unique record of the events, recorded at the time by those involved. The next chapter tells the final instalment in, perhaps, the most romanticised and daring escape in Scottish history.

Speed, bonnie boat, like a bird on the wing,
Onward! the sailors cry;
Carry the lad that's born to be king
Over the sea to Skye.

Loud the winds howl, loud the waves roar,
Thunderclaps rend the air;
Baffled, our foes stand by the shore,
Follow they will not dare.

Speed, bonnie boat, like a bird on the wing,
Onward! the sailors cry;
Carry the lad that's born to be king
Over the sea to Skye.

Many's the lad, fought on that day
Well the claymore did wield;

When the night came, silently lay
Dead on Culloden's field.

Speed, bonnie boat, like a bird on the wing,
Onward! the sailors cry;
Carry the lad that's born to be king
Over the sea to Skye.

Though the waves leap, soft shall ye sleep,
Ocean's a royal bed.
Rocked in the deep, Flora will keep
Watch by your weary head.

Speed, bonnie boat, like a bird on the wing,
Onward! the sailors cry;
Carry the lad that's born to be king
Over the sea to Skye.

Burned are their homes, exile and death
Scatter the loyal men;
Yet ere the sword cool in the sheath
Charlie will come again.

THE KING OVER THE WATER
(PART TWO)

Neil MacEachen was an experienced agent and recorded the events of that evening's escape in his journal, carefully written in the third person to deflect suspicion. An edited summary, here, clearly details the dangers of the scheme:

The prince at the same time was ordered to dress in woman's close (clothes), *that he might pass for her servant-maid, and Neil was appointed to take care of both. The scheme pleased the prince mightily, and he seemed very impatient to see it put in execution.*

The prince remained at the top of the hill the whole day. About sunset the prince told Neil that he entrusted himself into his hands, and that his life and safety depended upon him, Neil answered that the charge was more than what his life was worth; but yet, with God's assistance that he would find means to preserve him from all danger till every-thing was got ready to leave the country. After this they took a refreshment of bread-and-cheese, and set out towards the north end of the country, every-body carrying his own share of the baggage, the prince carried his own few shirts, O'Neill carried his own linen, and Neil carried the provisions, his own gun and sword, and the prince's fuses and one of his holsters, while the other hung upon his own belt. As they were going on, the prince clapt

*Neil's shoulder, often telling him if ever it was their good fortune
to get free of their present troubles, he would make him live easie
all his days for the fatigue of that night. Neil was informed some
days before, that Miss Flora lived with her brother in a glen near
Locheynort.*

*When the prince was informed of it, he wished to go and see her,
and tell her of the message he had from her stepfather. When they
were near the little house where she was asleep, for her brother was
not at home, Neil left the prince and O'Neill at a distance off, 'till
he went in and wakened her; she got scarcely on the half of her close*
(clothes), *when the prince, with his baggage upon his back, was
at the door, and saluted her very kindly; after which she brought
to him a part of the best cheer she had, among the rest was given
a large bowl full of creme, of which he took two or three hearty go-
downs, and his fellow-travellers swallowed the rest.*

*The prince, stript of his own clothes, was dressed by Miss Flora in
his new attire, but could not keep his hands from adjusting his
head dress, which he cursed a thousand times. There they lay till
the evening, waiting impatiently for the night, to set off. Here they
were alarmed by five wherries* (boats), *the same, as they supposed,
that had landed the Campbells the night before in Benbecula,
supposing, by taking this precaution, to keep the prince from
making his escape. But their fears were soon over; for the wherries
sailed by to the southward without ever stopping. After sunset they
got into their boat, which was managed by the following persons
- Rory McDonald, John McDonald, John McMurich, Duncan
Campbell, and Rory McDonald of Glengary family; the prince
passed for Miss McDonald's maid, and Neil McDonald in the
quality of a servant.*

The weather proving calm in the beginning of the night, they rowed away at a good rate .... The prince, who, all this time, was not in the least discouraged, encouraged them to row still better, saying that he would relieve him that was most fatigued. The poor men, almost ready to breathe out their last, at length made the point of Watersay on the north corner of the Isle of Skye, where, having got into a cliff by a rock, they rested themselves for an hour, and at the same time revived their drooping spirits with a plentiful repast of bread and butter, while the water that fell from the top of the rock furnished them drink.

This gave them fresh vigour for to undertake the remaining part of their labour . . . they landed in Kilbride in Trotternish (the northernmost peninsula on the Isle of Skye) *within a cannon shot of Sir Alexander Macdonald's house.*

In the neighbourhood of this place was another party of the Skye militia, who was post'd there to examine all boats that came from the isles, as they were pretty well assured that the prince was there at that time. Miss Flora and Neil having kept the prince in the boat as well as they could, went to the house, leaving strict orders with the boatmen not to stir from it till they came back, or some word from them, and in case their curiosity led any-body thither, who might perhaps take the liberty to ask who was the person kept in the boat, to answer Miss McDonald's maid, and to curse her for a lazy jade, what was she good for, since she did not attend her Mrs.

About an hour before sunset they set off for Kingsborough, where they were to be that night. Miss Flora, who staid for dinner at Mungstot, that she might not be suspected by Lieut. MacLeod, followed on horseback at some distance, and was mightily diverted to hear several of the country people with whom she fell in upon the

*road, as they returned from the meeting house at Mungstot, make
their remarks upon the behaviour of Betty Burke, her maid, which
name the prince borrowed when he left the Isle of Uist.*

*Neil, who walked a little behind the prince, and hearing the subject
the fellows were upon, went slower till they came up and joined
him, but they, notwithstanding, continued to speak with the same
freedom as before, of the impudence and assurance of Miss Burke,
who was not ashamed to walk and keep company with the men.
Betty, very easie of what would be said of her, went on always
at such a rate, that she very often got a piece before her fellow
travellers, which gave occasion to some of the fellows to cry out,
'Curse the wretch do you observe, sir, what terrible steps she takes,
how manly she walks, how carelessly she carries her dress' and a
hundred such like expressions, which they repeated over and over
again.*

Prince Charles Stuart was still disguised as Betty Burke
when the party reached the house of Macdonald of
Kingsburgh. Forgetting that he was still in disguise as an
Irish maid, the prince greeted Lady Macdonald. She would
describe the strange creature that greeted her as, *'an old
muckle trollop of a carlin, making lang wide steps through the
hall.'* (A 'carlin' was a derogatory expression, meaning a
haggard old witch!)

On the evening of 29th June, the prince, accompanied by
a guide, started for Portree, briefly stopping in a wood
to change his female clothing for traditional Highland
dress. The prince then took his leave of Flora, giving her a
locket containing his miniature portrait, thanking her, and

expressing an earnest wish that they might meet again one day. He was never to see her again.

An extraordinary two-month period was about to begin, in which the Young Pretender managed to elude capture, sometimes by the skin of his teeth, while British troops tightened their grip on the countryside.

He stayed briefly in Portree (even drinking in a public house), then sailed to the island of Raasay, but feared the island was too small and narrow for effective concealment, so he returned to Skye in a boat, attended by John MacLeod, Murdoch MacLeod (his brother), Malcolm MacLeod, and two boatmen. They came ashore at night at Nicolson's Rock, near Scorobreck, and spent an uncomfortable night in a cow-byre.

On 4th July, the prince and four boatmen embarked in a boat for the mainland. Malcolm MacLeod, who stayed behind, was taken prisoner by the militia. Finally, Charles arrived at Mallaig, on Loch Nevis, in the early morning of the 5th July, and slept for three nights in the open air, before taking to the hills to avoid redcoat troops they had witnessed patrolling on Loch Nevis.

Two more exhausting months were to follow for the prince, in which he was forced to hide in damp caves, sleep rough in open fields, narrowly escape falling over a precipice, disguise himself as 'Mr Sinclair', a ship-wrecked merchant, dodge government troops – sometimes by a matter of yards – and endure huge pangs of hunger (forcing his party to shoot stags and game wherever they could). Finally, after countless days of hardship, countless midge bites and thistle

stings, the prince reached the remote shores of Loch nan
Uamh, on the west coast, late on the evening of Monday
19th September. Here, waiting for him, lay the French vessel
Du Teillay. The prince, and a large number of his followers,
boarded the ship and, under cover of darkness, shortly
after midnight on Tuesday 20th September 1746 the ship
weighed anchor and silently sailed away out of sight and on
to France.

A full 156 days had passed since the prince had escaped
from the aftermath of Culloden. Many had risked their lives
to help him, losing their property, their liberty, or their lives
in the process. The Jacobite rebellion was in tatters and the
iron fist of punitive British justice held the Highlands in its
vice-like grip.

With the prince now absconded to France, and the Jacobite resistance crushed, what became of the key protagonists in this story, not to mention the legendary lost Jacobite gold?

Flora MacDonald, along with the boatmen involved in the prince's escape, was arrested soon afterwards. She was imprisoned at Dunstaffnage Castle, near Oban, and then taken to the Tower of London. On 12th July 1746 she confessed and dictated a statement detailing her part in the affair, which is now held by the National Records of Scotland:

Miss F McDonald, Daughter in Law of McDonald of Milton in Skye, being, by General Campbell's order, made Prisoner for assisting the eldest son [Bonnie Prince Charlie] of the Pretender in his escape from South Uist, & asked to declare the Circumstances thereof...

Following a full description of the escape she completed her declaration by confirming that she possessed no knowledge of the prince's current location.

On the 30th of June, Miss MacDonald set out on horseback from Kingsbury's House for Portree, having first desired the Young Pretender might put on his own clothes somewhere on the road to Portree, as she had observed that the other dress rather made him more suspected. Miss F got to Portree about 12: at night, where she found Donald MacDonald, who had been sent before to procure a Boat, then the Young Pretender & MacAncran arrived about an hour. Here the Young Pretender took some Refreshment, changed a Guinea, paid the Reckoning (bill), took his Leave of Miss MacDonald & went out with Donald MacDonald, but who, after seeing him to the Boat returned. She believes he went to Rasay

(Raasay, an island located between the Isle of Skye and the mainland of Scotland), *but cannot tell what is become of him since.*

Perhaps surprisingly, Flora MacDonald was not badly treated by the British authorities. She was eventually released under the *Act of Indemnity* in 1747 and returned to Syke. On 6th November 1750, she married Allan MacDonald, a captain in the British Army. The couple were even visited by the writer and Jacobite sympathiser Samuel Johnson in 1773 during his visit to the island.

The couple emigrated to North Carolina, where Allan fought on the side of the British in the American War of Independence. He was imprisoned for 18 months. Following his release, the couple eventually returned to Skye, where they managed to live out their remaining years in reasonable financial security, thanks mainly to their third son, John, who had made his fortune in India. Flora died in 1790 at the age of 68 and was buried in Kilmuir Cemetery, her husband followed in 1792. The couple had seven surviving children, two daughters and five sons, two of whom were lost at sea during the 1780s. Samuel Johnson was asked to pen the inscription on Flora's memorial at Kilmuir, 'a name that will be mentioned in history, and if courage and fidelity be virtues, mentioned with honour'.

The Duke of Cumberland, better known as Prince William Augustus KG, KB, FRS, or 'Butcher Cumberland', was the third and youngest son of King George II. He was given the title Duke of Cumberland from 1726, while aged just five years old. Although, perhaps, best remembered for his role in crushing the Jacobite Rising at the Battle of

Culloden (an act which made him immensely popular throughout parts of lowland Scotland and England) he had a largely unsuccessful military career. Perhaps, even more remarkably, his epithet 'Butcher' was, in fact, one given to him by his Tory opponents in England, and not by the fleeing Jacobite soldiers in the aftermath of Culloden.

After a military career on the continent and in North America, which met with only varying degrees of success, he turned his hand to politics and horse racing. However, his popularity and his health also waned. The duke never fully recovered from a wound inflicted at the Battle of Dettingen, in what is now Bavaria. He suffered a stroke in 1760, complicated by his obesity, and passed away on 31st October 1765, at his home on Upper Grosvenor Street in London, aged just 44.

What happened to the Young Pretender following his escape from Scotland? The prince, or to give him his full name, Charles Edward Louis John Casimir Sylvester Severino Maria Stuart, always hoped to return triumphantly to Scotland. Alas, this was never to occur. In 1748, the war between France and England ended and the English insisted that the French exile Charles. He was forced to spend the rest of his life roaming across Europe in a range of guises. After the defeat at Culloden, Charles indicated to his remaining supporters that he fully accepted the impossibility of his ever recovering the Crown of England and Scotland, while still remaining a Roman Catholic. The prince informed his supporters that he was willing to commit himself to reigning as a Protestant. With this in mind he visited London in secret during 1750 and converted to the Protestant faith by receiving an Anglican communion.

Charles lived for several years in European exile with his Scottish mistress, Clementina Walkinshaw, whom he had met, and possibly begun a relationship with, during the '45 rebellion. In 1753, the couple had a daughter, Charlotte. However, his inability to deal with the collapse of the Jacobite cause led to problems with alcohol, and eventually Clementina and his daughter left him. By the age of 45, Charles had few supporters and was excluded from his father's will.

In 1772 he married a nineteen-year-old bride, but, following another breakdown, forced her into a Convent. From 1783 onwards, the prince, now residing in Rome, became seriously ill and was nursed by his daughter until 1788, when he suffered a stroke. He passed away on 31st January, at the age of 68, never fulfilling his wish to return to Scotland or to meet Flora MacDonald again.

Yet, despite the death of their rightful heir to the throne, clandestine Jacobite clubs continued well into the nineteenth century, long after any hope of a Stuart restoration had gone. Diehard supporters of Charles, captivated by the mystery and romance of the rebellions, met in secret and toasted 'the King over the water', by passing their glasses over a vessel containing water, such as a finger bowl. Such was the perceived potency of these words that the authorities made any such toast, and even the possession of Jacobite drinking glasses, a treasonable offence. The provision of finger bowls at official functions was even delayed until after loyal Hanoverian toasts had been drunk, in order to prevent any Jacobite sympathisers present from secretly honouring their cause.

There are, perhaps, two questions that have intrigued historians, and those captivated with the story of the Jacobite rebellion, above all others.

Firstly, what became of the lost Jacobite gold, designed to finance the campaign against the British forces? And, secondly, would the outcome at Culloden have been any different had the war chest of louis d'or coins arrived earlier?

The search for clues to the existence and hiding place of the lost gold began in my earlier book, *Blood Beneath Ben Nevis*. Since its publication in 2020, there are several updates to the story, which are covered in later chapters of this current book.

The second question, regarding the possibility of a fully financed Jacobite army being victorious at Culloden, is, of course, a hypothetical one. In all probability, the short period of time between the arrival of the French gold and the battle would not have compensated for the manpower shortage, the strategic mistakes, and the lack of direction shown by the Jacobite leadership on the battlefield. Nor would it have adequately offset the Jacobite's lack of cavalry in the face of the well-trained British dragoons, which led to the slaughter of so many Highland musketeers under the blade of the charging cavalrymen.

Nevertheless, if the rebellion had succeeded despite the overwhelming odds, it is almost certain Scotland would have become an independent nation in 1746.

THE PROBLEM WITH MURDER
(PART ONE)

The majority of killings tend not to be premeditated, but instead are the result of a momentary aberration or tragic accident. In these cases, a defendant must rely on the mercy of the jury. However, in the case of a more carefully planned and premeditated murder, the dilemma facing the killer is not just that of committing the act, it is the practical difficulty in concealing their guilt, both before and after the act.

The authorities, of course, face a very different problem; proving a suspect's guilt to the satisfaction of a jury. Today that task is made easier, largely thanks to improvements in forensic science, fingerprinting, CCTV, and DNA analysis. Yet, despite the huge resources that can now be levelled in a murder inquiry, even today, only about half of all murders are actually solved.

Two centuries ago, the task was a far more onerous one. Often, there was little available evidence with which to secure a conviction, other than that which might now be called circumstantial. In addition, successful prosecutions for murder often hinged purely on the whims of the all-male juries.

Perhaps no case better demonstrates these problems
than the prosecution of Alexander Macdougall for the
horrific and protracted death of his wife Sophia Agnes
Macdougall during March 1877. Alexander Macdougall
was widely expected to face the hangman's noose for the
crime. However, in Scotland, where juries were notoriously
reluctant to send a man to the gallows, there was every
chance he might escape the gallows. Indeed, so confident
was Macdougall when arrested, he taunted the police,
saying, 'You may as well let me go now; no good Scottish
jury will hang me.'

Alexander Macdougall, aged 39, was the innkeeper and
landlord of Kingshouse Hotel, nestled in the shadow of
Buachaille Etive Mor, the mountain known as 'the watcher
of the moor', situated halfway between the village of
Glencoe and Bridge of Orchy. Macdougall was a fearsome
man; hot-tempered, intimidating and invariably drunk. His
behaviour was, however, anything but predictable. At any
moment he might change from the jovial innkeeper into
a violent drunkard and a 'man who was overcome with a
maniacal fit of frenzy', as one witness would later describe
him.

One bitterly cold February day in 1877, James Cameron,
a local shepherd, was driving his horse and cart along
the rough track from Ballachulish to Kinghouse Hotel,
intending to stop for a drink. As he approached, he noticed
a half-naked man staggering towards him. The man, who
he recognised as Alexander Macdougall, was wearing just
an open shirt, with no trousers or boots, and his bare feet

were red raw in the snow. Macdougall had a shotgun in his right hand.

Looking menacingly at James Cameron, Macdougall asked him, 'Come with me to the shooting.'

'I cannot. I am going to Kinghouse for a drink,' Cameron replied.

'Accompany me to the shooting or you'll get a belly full o' my gun. I insist!'

Thinking quickly, Cameron responded, 'I will go, if you can get a gun for me to use.'

Macdougall agreed and turned to walk back to the hotel to fetch another weapon. With that, James Cameron grabbed the reins and drove his horse as fast as possible; past the hotel, around Loch Tulla, past the great white summits of Stob Ghabhar and Aonach Mor, through Bridge of Orchy, and finally to the comparative safety of Tyndrum. A sizeable distance to travel in the grip of winter on Rannoch Moor.

Nevertheless, later that evening, as Cameron sat warming himself in the bar of the inn at Tyndrum, Alexander Macdougall suddenly appeared in the doorway and threatened everyone in the room with a loaded revolver. Several of Macdougall's acquaintances, who happened to be present, persuaded him to lower the weapon; nevertheless, the event left many certain that Macdougall's 'sense of reason had temporarily left him' and that he was 'a man, frenzied and insane.'

It would only be a matter of weeks until Macdougall's explosive temper and fragile sanity finally reached breaking point. However, due to the remoteness of the region, it would be three weeks until the full horror of the events reached a shocked public, as this article from the *Dundee Evening Telegraph* reports:

30th March 1877.

THE ALLEGED WIFE MURDER GLENCOE
SPECIAL ACCOUNT OF THE TRAGEDY

We are able today to publish the full particulars of a foul crime, committed nearly three weeks ago, which has shocked the inhabitants of this wide expanse of western Perthshire and the northern part of Argyllshire.

King's House Inn, the scene of the tragedy, is situated at the base of Buachaille Etive, the high mountain which separates the Glens of the Coe and Etive. The spot is one the most desolate in Scotland. With the exception of the inn, and two shepherds' huts close by, there is no human habitation for miles. Even in summer the place has a cheerless look, but in winter the prospect is dismal in the extreme. Coaching is stopped when the cold weather sets in, and letters are got only when sent for from Ballachulish, sixteen miles distant down Glencoe. The inn door stands close to the bridge that carries the road across the river. More than 100 years old, the two-storey inn was used to accommodate Royalist troops during the 1745 uprisings

To fully understand the narrative which follows, it is necessary to explain that on entering the main door there is a long, badly-lighted

*room on the left hand and, from that, a passage leads to a sitting
room, a sleeping room for tramps, which has a backdoor. To the
right of the entrance is a lobby leading to the kitchen, a bar and a
bedroom. At the end of the kitchen is a door leading out to the back
of the premises.*

*The upper floor contains a parlour with a bedroom attached, while
on the right side is a large bedroom. A passage leads to the back of
the house, terminating in another bedroom, which commands a
view of Buachaille Etive.*

*Seven years ago this inn was taken on a yearly lease from the Earl
of Breadalbane by Alexander Macdougall, a native of Kinghallin
in Kenmore. A man of superior education and intelligence,
who had for fifteen years been teacher at the Free Church school
at Killin, the duties of which he discharged with much ability.
In 1871 he married Miss Sophia Jarratt, the daughter of the
hotelkeeper at Dalmally.*

*The marriage was not a happy one, and differences followed
soon after the wedding. Macdougall is said to have been of sullen
and jealous disposition, while his wife was young, amiable,
and light-hearted. There was also much disparity in their years*
(Macdougall was six years older than his wife). *Frequent
bickerings took place. These soon developed into open quarrels, and
acts of violence on the part of the husband. Of course, this could
not go on for long without becoming known and it was evident to
all that the domestic arrangements were very inharmonious.*

*A little girl, the only issue of their marriage, was sent to live with
relatives in Edinburgh to be out of the way of the scenes that now
frequently occurred in the lonely dwelling. Mrs Macdougall also left
and took refuge with the neighbouring shepherds' wives to escape, it
is alleged, from the violence of her husband.*

This long course of quarrelling and ill-treatment culminated in a most tragic manner. Shortly after the New Year, Mrs Macdougall left King's House to take shelter at her brother's farm near Killin, and, although solicited not to return, she resolved to go back, saying she would make another trial of it. It proved to be her last.

According to information gathered, there was a terrible scene in the King's House on Monday, 12th March. Present at that time were Macdougall, his wife, a servant girl, and two post-boys named Alex Macgregor and 'Wee Donald'. Macdougall, inflamed by passion and drink - for drink was at the bottom of much of the violence and quarrelling - put everyone out of the house except his wife, and then barred the door. What followed was seen only by Macdougall and his unfortunate wife. There are various accounts as to what took place. The version on which we place most credence is that of the two boys, Macgregor and Donald, who, suspecting all was not right, tried to re-enter the house some ten days later. Finding the front door barred, they gained admission by the backdoor leading to the hall. This hall and the kitchen are separated by an unplastered partition, which, by breaking away the lathing, the boys managed to scramble in. In the lobby leading to the kitchen a sickening spectacle met their gaze. Underneath the window, opposite the door of the bar lay Mrs Macdougall, perfectly nude, her head in a pool of blood, and with injuries on various parts of her person. Mr Macdougall was in the bar with his clothes off.

The two boys, shocked at the terrible sight, unbarred the front door, and ran to the two shepherds' houses. They returned with the shepherds' wives, but they found the door again barred, but not securely, for with a push the bolt gave way.

Upon re-entering, it was found that Mrs Macdougall had been removed, evidently dragged along the floor, to the kitchen, where she lay with many injuries, her head smeared with blood, a deep cut on the right eye, and a wound on the left. Blood still marked the wall in the lobby where the body was first seen, and there were splashes on the kitchen door; and on the floor. Lying on the floor, beside the body, was found a watch-chain belonging to Macdougall.

Speedily they carried up the poor woman, placed her in bed, and did what they could to allay the pain of her wounds, which it is said, could not have been self-inflicted. Although at times sensible, she never recovered full consciousness, and died on the afternoon of Wednesday, 21ˢᵗ March, after lingering ten or so days. She was reported to have said before she died, 'If I get the better of this bad turn, I will leave him never to come back.'

While his wife lay dying, Macdougall went about his ordinary duties. No medical assistance was sent for until some days after the poor woman's death, when, either from word sent by Macdougall, or by the shepherds' wives, the doctor from Ballachulish arrived.

Meanwhile, rumours that Mrs Macdougall had met a violent death reached Mr MacLullich at Inveraray, the Procurator-Fiscal for Argyllshire, who instructed Constable MacEwan, on duty at Dalmally, to proceed to King's House to make inquiries. MacEwan reached King's House on Sunday, where, after making investigations, arrested Macdougall, to which Macdougall replied, 'Well, I will go with you quietly.'

He was taken to the cells at Dalmally, where his only request was that a candle should be left burning beside him all night. Next day he was conveyed to Inveraray, and under examination before

Sheriff-Substitute Sir George Home, he pleaded 'not guilty', and was committed to prison to await further inquiry.

Alexander Macdougall's previous conduct, and his feelings towards his wife, were well known. Following his questioning at Inveraray Jail, in which he openly declared his hatred for his wife's behaviour, Macdougall was charged as follows:

Alexander Macdougall, you are charged with the murder of your wife, Sophia Agnes Jarratt, or Macdougall, at King's House, in the parish of Glenorchy and Innishael, on the 21ˢᵗ of March last. That you, the prisoner did strike her repeated blows with your fist, or some other weapon, and kicked her repeatedly on or about the face, head, and dragged her about the floor of said house, by which she was mortally wounded, and in consequence of which she died, and was thus murdered by you, and that for several months you did evince (publicly declare) *your malice against your wife by repeatedly beating and assaulting her.*

Macdougall's poor stewardship of the hotel, coupled with its previous seedy character, had already given the King's House a notorious reputation. The poet Dorothy Wordsworth had visited in 1803, writing a scathing entry in her journal:

Never did I see such a miserable, wretched place - no other furniture except benches. The floors far dirtier than an ordinary house would be if it were never washed. After an hour of waiting, supper came, a shoulder of mutton so hard that it was impossible to chew the little flesh that might have been scraped off the bones.

Disturbing stories were also reported by travellers staying at the hotel. In 1876 a guest had died from (what was described as) 'hard drinking'. Rumours circulated that a permanent tenant at King's House had drunk himself to death. Older residents of Glencoe recalled the last execution at Inveraray, sixty years earlier, when a hawker named Macdougall, who was rumoured to be an ancestor of Alexander Macdougall, had murdered his wife by throwing her over the bridge which spans the River Etive outside the hotel. Many spoke of an insane streak in Macdougall's family, and others of strange, ghostly sightings of soldiers nearby.

Meanwhile, a trial date was set for Monday 16th July 1877 at the High Court of Justiciary in Edinburgh. Lord Justice-Clerk, Lord Moncrieff, presided. Mr Burnet QC was appointed to prosecute the case and Macdougall's defence was to be conducted by Macintosh and Gillespie Solicitors, who advised their client to enter a plea of insanity. Macdougall's assets were immediately sequestered, then sold, to pay the considerable costs of his defence.

In the meantime, the funeral of Sophia Macdougall took place in the quiet churchyard of the tranquil, octagonal parish church in the village of Dalmally. Only a small company of immediate relatives were present. Sophia Macdougall's coffin was conveyed on its solemn journey of twenty-six miles in an open shooting brake carriage and her name added to the unusual iron headstone.

Macdougall was transported by prison wagon from Inveraray Jail to face trial. It was a pleasant, sunny day in

Edinburgh and the large crowd jeered as the accused man was bundled inside the courthouse. Asked how he wished to plead, Macdougall seemed hugely affected by the occasion and his initial plea was mumbled so inaudibly that he was asked to repeat himself. Finally, his plea of not guilty was entered and the trial commenced.

The first witnesses to be examined by the prosecution were Sir George Home, Sheriff-Substitute of Argyll, and Mr A Mackay, the Chief Constable, who both deponed that Macdougall had made several statements while being questioned, 'during which time he was in sound and sober senses.'

The next witness to be called, Mrs Margaret Macdonald, was only able to speak in Gaelic, and spoke through the Court's interpreter, Mr Malcolm Nicolson She testified that:

Lately I was a servant of the prisoner. There were no other servants but myself and two post-boys. The nearest other house to the inn was the shepherd's house about a mile away. Mr Macdougall and his wife slept in the bar, which was next to the kitchen. He was drinking on Saturday the 10th of March, and Mrs Macdougall commenced drinking on the Sunday, but only a drop.

Mr Burnet enquired, *And was that the first time you had witnessed them drinking, Mrs Macdonald?*

Mrs Macdougall replied, *No, they had been often drinking before.*

And when did you suspect that the deceased might have come to some harm?

I observed marks on Mrs Macdougall's body nine days before, on her forehead and back. She had a cut on the forehead and her back was bruised. Also, shortly before her death I heard them quarrelling.

Was that the first time you had heard them quarrelling?

No sir, frequently I heard them, and for a long time.

Their quarrels were long lasting then?

Aye, now and again, sir.

Mr Gillespie, for the defence, then cross-examined the witness, *Did you ever actually see Mr Macdougall strike his wife?*

No, I never saw a blow struck. I was called frequently in, though, by Mrs Macdougall, but he did not strike her if I was present.

So, you never actually saw my client strike or raise a hand to his wife?

No, sir.

And did you not ask him about his wife's bruises?

No... '

Thank you, **Mr Gillespie** interrupted Mrs Macdonald before she could finish her answer, *that will be all.*

Mr Burnet then continued for the prosecution, *And did you not enquire from Mrs Macdougall as to how she acquired such terrible bruises?*

I did, sir. I remember speaking to her, and she said it was her husband who did it. This was a considerable time before her death. More than once or twice, I seen marks on her face.

And how did the prisoner explain to others, these rather obvious marks upon his wife's face?

Well, sir, he once asked me what had happened to her; and said that he had no definite idea what could have caused the marks.

And you did not challenge his remarks, Mrs Macdonald?

No, sir, I was frightened of Mr Macdougall and so was Mrs Macdougall. About six weeks before her death I noticed that the top of her ear had been cut off and it was festering.

And did Mrs Macdougall explain how that injury had occurred?'

No, she did not say, and I did not ask her.

And what happened next, Mrs Macdonald?

On the night of the 11th of March, they were both very bad with drink. But when she had drink she was quiet and gentle, and went off to her bed. But if was interfering with her she was quarrelsome.

And what happened on the morning of the 12th March, Mrs Macdonald?

*She seemed quite well that morning. About eight o'clock, I was
coming in from the byre, when I heard one of the young boys calling
out for me. When I got into the kitchen, I found Mrs Macdougall
had come in for water. Mr Macdougall followed her into the kitchen
and dragged her back into the bar. Mrs Macdougall called out for
me to help, but Mr Macdougall tried to push me out. She begged me
to stay; and I intended to because I was afraid he might hurt her.*

And then what happened?

*He forced me out and so I went to the shepherd's house. The two
young lads were left in the house. At the time I left there was
nothing wrong with the face of Mrs Macdougall. Next, one of the
boys came to fetch me. He told me that my mistress was calling for
me. With Mrs Cameron, the shepherd's wife, I went back to King's
House and went in by the back door and through to the kitchen.
My mistress was lying in the kitchen, stark naked as if she were
dead. Her apron was full of blood, I could not see where it came
from. We then lifted her into the bed.*

And was Mrs Macdougall still alive at this point?

*I could not say whether she was alive or dead. I met Mr
Macdougall at the door, and I was put out by him, so I went
away back to Mrs Cameron's house. The next morning one of
the post boys, Alex MacGregor, came for me and I went back to
King's House. Mrs Macdougall was still in her bed. She asked me
to give her a chemise as she was still naked. Her brow was cut. It
was swelled bad. Her head, shoulders and legs were scratched and
bruised also, and nothing had been done in the way of dressing her
wounds. I spoke to my mistress, and she didn't tell me how it had*

happened. A doctor was called in. He moved Mrs Macdougall from her bed to my bed and I wiped up the blood in the bar.

And where was Mr Macdougall at this point?

He was there. He offered me a whisky, but I would not take it from his hands. He did not say anything, and he did not explain the state my mistress was in. I noticed two marks, like scratches, on his face. He would not say how they came to be there.

At this juncture, Mr Burnet pointed out to the jury that:

Among the chemises afterwards found by the police, the one which the deceased was wearing on that day was not found, and it has not been found since.

At this stage, the prosecution's evidence seemed irresistible. Could the defence advocate limit the damage to his client's case?

THE PROBLEM WITH MURDER
(PART TWO)

Mr Gillespie stood up to cross-examine on behalf of the defence, *Is it true, Mrs Macdonald, that when your mistress is the worse for drink, she usually keeps it up for some time? And is it also true that they lived quietly enough together when sober?*

Mrs Macdougall only had a drop of wine from the 12th to her death, as far as I know.

And you say that a doctor was called for. How close is the nearest doctor?

Thirteen miles away.

And are there any steps from the kitchen to the bar passage, Mrs Macdonald?

Yes, there are three steps.

And what is the floor?

It is stone flags, sir.

And could Mrs Macdougall's injuries have been caused by falling, or tripping, on these steps while intoxicated?

Well, sir, I have never...

A simple 'yes' or 'no' will suffice.

Yes, I suppose, but...

Thank you, Mrs Macdonald. And did your mistress not say to you that she was too drunk to remember how she had been hurt?

I don't remember that, sir.

Very well. And did Mr Macdougall have boots on, on the day of the alleged assault?

No, sir. He was in his stockinged feet. He had not been out as far as I knew.

Then, if he did not have his boots on, it is not likely that he could have caused her injuries with his feet, is it, Mrs Macdonald?

At this point Mr Burnet interrupted the defence's cross-examination on behalf of the prosecution, *Objection, my Lord!*

Lord Moncrieff agreed and scolded the defence, *Mr Gillespie, the witness is here to tell us what she saw, not what she may think, or what you wish her to say.* There was a stifled laugh in the courtroom.

My apologies, my Lord, replied the defence barrister. *Thank you, Mrs Macdonald, that will be all.*

The prosecution continued. Four further witnesses were called, Donald MacLeish, a gamekeeper in Glen Coe, Alex Cameron, the shepherd, and his wife, followed by Margaret Dewar, a former employee of Mr Macdougall. All the witnesses testified to having seen Sophia Macdougall with cuts and bruises about her face. All three also recalled having challenged Mr Macdougall regarding his treatment of his wife. Donald MacLeish testified to the court:

The master and mistress were sometimes addicted to drink, and I often noticed bruises on her face. Two-or-three times Mr Macdougall said to me, "I wonder how she got those?" and I answered that I did not know. Once, about the New Year, I saw her limping, she was lame, like a horse. Then, on the day after she died, I found a chemise, with blood still on it, in the river, and I brought it to the prisoner and told him that it was his poor wife's. I have not seen it since.

Next, Mrs Cameron, the shepherd's wife, detailed her conversations with Sophia Macdougall:

She told me that if she got better she would leave him and go to her uncle and aunt. I once saw him get out of bed for no other reason than to strike Mrs Macdougall repeatedly, when she was quite sober and only writing out a receipt for rent. She had given him no provocation. I never saw her touched with drink, except in bed, four or five times. She never took a drop in my company.

Next came the crucial evidence of the post boy, Alex MacGregor, who was asked:

Can you explain to the court what happened when you first saw your mistress on the kitchen floor?

We lifted her from the floor and carried her into bed.

And did you notice anything of a peculiar nature?

Well, sir, I found Mr Macdougall's watch-chain, which had been lying under her.

That is unusual. Thank you. And what did you do then?

Mr Macdougall came into the kitchen, and he had no coat, trousers, or shoes on. He asked me where his wife was, and I said she had been taken into the pantry bed. I said something to him about the house they were keeping, and the way he had used the mistress.

That was very brave of you remarked Mr Burnet, *How did the prisoner reply?*

Mr Macdougall was angry at that and said he didn't do anything of the sort. I told him to go away to his bed, or something like that. After that, the master put us all out of house and bolted all the doors. He was alone with her in the house until the day about two weeks later when we climbed in and let the police in the door. She was dead and Mr Macdougall was sat in the bar alone and undressed.'

And had you seen this kind of incident before that night?

Aye, sir. I have, and I have seen Mrs Macdougall with black eyes before.

Again, Mr Gillespie desperately attempted to limit the damage to his client, and forthrightly questioned the young post boy, *Mr MacGregor, have you ever seen my client attempting to keep drink away from his wife?*

Yes, I believe he has tried before.

And did that cause quarrelling between the couple?

I believe so.

And is it also true that during the previous winter, when she was drinking heavily, my client put her in a room upstairs, and locked the door? And that Mrs Macdougall then took the poker and forced up the window, and fell out of it into the snow? Could not this fall have caused her previous injuries, rather than an attack of some sort?

Alex MacGregor reluctantly agreed that it was possible.

Tell me, Mr MacGregor, did you ever see my client strike his wife?

No, but…

Mr Gillespie did not allow the young post boy to qualify his answer, *Thank you. Members of the jury, this witness has confirmed to you that he did NOT see Mr Macdougall strike his wife. Ever.* He continued, *It has also been suggested by my learned friend for the prosecution that my client was particular about keeping the doors locked. Do you know why that was?*

No, I do not know, sir.

Might I suggest to you that my client kept the doors locked merely to keep drink from his wife, and it was that which caused her to quarrel with him? in fact, I will go further, Did Mrs Macdougall not jump out of the window of the bedroom, not once, but twice, in search of hard drink?

There were disapproving murmurs from the gallery as Mr
Gillespie challenged the Crown's case, using his imposing
personality to intimidate the young post boy. Undeterred,
he continued:

*Now we come to the question of the watch-chain which you claim to
have found under the deceased's body. My client assures me that his
watch and chain were at that time at a watchmakers in Edinburgh
for repair. So, I put it to you that perhaps you were mistaken; or
that you saw the watch-chain at some other time?*

I saw the watch-chain, sir.

*But can you be sure it was my client's? After all, do not all watch-
chains look much alike?*

I think it was.

*But you are not certain? Could you have mistaken it in the dim
light? Perhaps it was another's?*

I suppose so, but I think I am right.

But you only suppose, announced Mr Gillespie, before
turning to Lord Moncrieff, *I have no further questions, my
Lord, thank you.*

Margaret Dewar was next to be questioned by the
prosecution, *Mrs Dewar, I understand you are no longer in the
employ of the accused?*

*No sir, I left last year on account of what happened. In November, I
found Mrs Macdougall lying in a pool of blood. She told me it was
her husband that had done it; but he had made her promise not to*

tell. I once saw the prisoner strike his wife, and she had a black eye afterwards. Once, while her husband was still in the room, she said to me that an injury on her head had been caused by a fall; but, later, she said that was not true, and that he had done it with a brush.

Finally came the all-important medical testimony, to be given by Dr MacKelvie, from Oban, Dr Kennedy, from Fort William, and Dr MacCulloch from Ballachulish. The graphic and bloody nature of post-mortem evidence frequently caused gasps of disbelief from the public galleries, often resulting in ladies of a delicate disposition fainting, or being asked to leave the courtroom. This problem did not extend to the jury, however, as female jurors were not permitted until the passing of the *Sex Disqualification (Removal) Act 1919*. Indeed, it was often thought that an all-male jury might aid the defence of a man charged with the murder of an unsympathetic female victim.

After the court had been cleared of ladies likely to faint on hearing the medical evidence, Dr MacKelvie began:

On 26th March, Dr Kennedy and myself were summoned to King's House by the Procurator-Fiscal. We were given to understand that a good deal of trouble had been undertaken to affect an entry into the building, as the property had been bolted from the inside; and as a consequence, it was some days until the authorities had been made aware of the death.

Only then were we able to perform an examination upon the body of Mrs Macdougall. Life appeared to have been extinct for about six days. The body was quite fresh, but it presented numerous wounds, bruises, and sores. Erysipelas (a bacterial skin infection) *had set in on one of the temples. We considered it likely that the fatal injuries were inflicted approximately two weeks earlier.*

The autopsy, in our opinion, indicated that death was caused by inflammation of the cellular membrane, and subsequent suppuration (the discharging of pus from a wound), *resulting from severe bruises. We noted a series of abrasions and bruises on different part of the legs, arms, hands, head, and face; and the tearing off of a part of the deceased's left ear, and a one-inch incised wound on the forehead.*

Are you able to state how these injuries might have occurred, Doctor?, enquired Lord Moncrieff.

The wounds on the legs might have been caused by falls or kicks, or the dragging over a stone floor of the naked body. It would require a good number of falls, however, to produce this appearance. The hair on the deceased's head was thinner on one side than upon the other, consistent with the hair having been pulled out. A small part of cartilage of the left ear and three-fourths of the skin of the same ear were removed, and the ear was in a suppurating state. There was considerable effusion and swelling over the left parietal and temporal bones, and a large swelling over the left cheek. Immediately below the left eye there was a skin discolouration. On cutting into the swelling over the parietal and temporal bones, a quantity of pus was released. In addition, there was a substantial abrasion on the victim's back, probably caused by being dragged across the stone floor, her back being in contact with the rough surface. Her thinning hair might also indicate that she was pulled by the hair.

The deceased's body was otherwise healthy, and no indications were found of chronic drinking or of death by suffocation.

Thank you, Doctor. What is your conclusion as to the actual cause of death?

It was our opinion that death resulted from diffuse cellulitis (a rapidly spreading streptococci infection) *produced by inflammation and subsequent suppuration from severe bruises on the face and head.*

Several members of the jury appeared distressed at the shocking nature of this evidence, and a short recess was granted by Lord Moncrieff, before Mr Gillespie began the case for the defence.

In 1877 the law did not normally allow the accused person to speak in their own defence at trial, a practice enshrined in Scottish common law since the seventeenth-century. Any effort by the prosecution to force a defendant to provide answers was considered unlawful. By the mid-1880s, the right to testify would be introduced in less serious cases. That right was eventually extended to all offences by 1898. However, the accused person's right to maintain silence was, and still is, clearly protected in law.

In this, as is many other contemporary cases, Mr Gillespie instead read out a sworn statement prepared earlier by Alexander Macdougall. As it was read to the court, the accused man sat in silence, his face turned towards the floor.

The prisoner has deponed to the following: 'I attributed her injuries to falls, which often occurred while she was under the influence

*of drink. I denied to the police that I had struck or injured
her. Regarding my not having sent earlier for the doctor; I had
repeatedly before seen her apparently low with drink, and I did not
see anything unusual in her condition. I often had the need to bolt
the door to keep her away from the drink, and she pushed me and
fought me to get past. The scratches on my forehead occurred when
I had struck my face against a door after she pushed me. My wife's
bruises were caused when she had fallen and got hurt while ill or
drunk'.*

Doctor MacKelvie was then recalled to the stand,

*Doctor, thank you for your most detailed evidence earlier. In my
understanding, the most serious injury was one over the left
parietal and temporal bones. There was discolouration of the skin
and swelling. However, the suppuration of the ear seemed to be of
old standing, and, indeed, might be some months in age. Where
you able to form an opinion as to the cause of that particular
injury?*

No.

*In fact, might this injury merely have been caused by the accidental
falls of a person staggering about, perhaps under the influence of
drink?*

It is certainly possible.

The defence then called Doctor MacCulloch.

*Doctor MacCulloch, have you attended Mrs Macdougall at any
time in the past?*

*I have attended the deceased twice for, what was thought to be,
delirium tremens - once in March 1875 and once since then.*

*Delirium tremens - commonly known as DTs - is characterised as
a rapid onset of confusion usually caused by withdrawal from
alcohol. Symptoms include shaking, shivering, and hallucinations.*

*She had the signs of a person much addicted to drink, when I last
attended her. I asked if her husband had done these things to her,
and she said no. She began to wander afterwards in her mind. At
first, I thought she was suffering from DTs, however, she was in a
very neglected state in bed at the time.*

*And did you think at the time that she understood your question
regarding who had left her in that state?*

Yes, I thought that she answered intelligently, replied Doctor
MacCulloch.

And did my client speak to you about his wife's condition?

*Yes, I spoke to Mr Macdougall about the matter, and he said that
it was likely people would think he was the cause of it, but that he
was quite innocent, and that it was drink that did it.*

Thank you, Doctor.

The next defence witness, Mrs Macdonald, described her
relationship to Mrs Macdougall and her time at Kinghouse:

*For two years I was in the service of Mr Macdougall. During that
time his wife drank a great deal, as long as she could get leave
to carry the drink away from her husband's sight. She often had
marks about her face; and tumbled when she was going about the
house. I once saw her fall against the mantelpiece and cut herself
above the eye. Sometimes she said her husband did it, and other
times she said she fell. He was as kind as he could be to her, when
she was sober.*

Finally, in a dramatic move, which created a buzz of anticipation in the courtroom, Mr Gillespie called his own medical witnesses. Both men were famous experts in their field and enjoyed considerable reputations. Dr Henry Littlejohn had served for almost fifty years as Edinburgh's first Medical Officer of Health, during which time he brought about significant improvements in the living conditions of the city's inhabitants. He also acted as an autopsy specialist for the Edinburgh City Police force, and as a medical adviser during many famous Scottish murder trials.

Doctor Joseph Bell was a Scottish surgeon and lecturer at the University of Edinburgh. He had recognised the importance of minute observation in making a diagnosis. His unique skills made Doctor Bell the first pioneer in the field of forensic pathology; and he would – most famously – become Sir Arthur Conan Doyle's real-life inspiration for the character of Sherlock Holmes.

Doctor Littlejohn, you have read the medical report in this case. Could you please give the court your opinion on its findings

I have examined the medical report and I can confirm that all the injuries, with the exception of the suppurating swelling on the side of the head, were on prominent and protruding parts of the body, and might well have been caused by falls. The suppurated swelling on the side of the deceased's head would, judging by the medical report, probably not have been caused by violence. It might, however, have been caused by a fall, particularly on a person with a diseased constitution. With the exception of this suppurated swelling, the other wounds were of a trivial description, and

*none of them, either singly or in combination, were likely, in the
ordinary person, to be mortal. The injuries, in my opinion, did not
completely account for the death; and there must have been some
other cause.*

Next, Doctor Joseph Bell gave his expert opinion:

*I have examined the evidence, and I can only conclude that, in
my judgement, the post-mortem examination was not conducted
with sufficient minuteness to discover the true cause of death. My
opinion on the facts stated in the medical reports, and the known
habits of the deceased, was that she died of chronic alcoholism. It
is also my opinion that there is nothing in the medical report to
account for the death of the deceased, and that there must have
been some other cause. It is impossible to say whether accident or
violence caused Mrs Macdougall's death, or if violence had taken
place, whether it was sufficient to cause death. There was also
the possibility of suffocation being the cause of death, through the
victim being too weak to clear her own throat.*

And with that revelation, the case for the defence closed.

Each side then gave their final summation of the evidence.

Mr Burnet, for the prosecution, addressed the jury
earnestly:

*I am asking the jury for a verdict of guilty in this case. It is clear
from the evidence that the previous history of these people made it
extremely likely that someday violence would be done to the deceased
which would result in her death. That much is certain. For months,
it was clear the prisoner had been guilty of behaviour, for which
no misconduct on the part of his wife could afford justification.
I cannot do my duty in this case without asking you to consider*

the evidence, with the view to returning the verdict of guilty which seems just in these circumstances. Thank you.

Mr Gillespie then delivered his impassioned plea for Alexander Macdougall:

For my client, there is, in the first place, no evidence at all that murder was intended, and that charge should be excluded from your minds. I submit, also, that the evidence here is totally insufficient to prove that my client inflicted his wife's injuries. Furthermore, it has been clearly established that these injuries, and her death also, were due to the results of her own intemperate habits. I earnestly implore that you find my client not guilty in this most difficult and distressing case.

Lord Moncrieff then instructed the jury:

A very lamentable and melancholy picture of domestic life has been put before you in this case. The issue put for your consideration, members of the jury, is of the gravest order. I will direct your attention to three crucial questions, being those on which you must base your decision. Firstly, whether the death of this unfortunate woman was or was not caused by violence? Secondly, whether, if she did, indeed, die from violence, whether the violence was the act of the accused? And, finally, whether the use of the violence by the accused, followed by death, amounted to the crime of murder or to something short of that crime.

You must review not only the medical evidence, but the evidence as to the circumstances which led up to the death. That this woman was a drunkard was beyond all doubt. Without any medical testimony, and solely on the evidence of witnesses, it is highly probable that a jury would not hesitate in concluding that these circumstances led to her death. If you think violence was the cause of death, or a contributory, but not the main, cause of death then you must consider the second question, whether she died from that violence.

On the point of whether the defendant was the cause of her injuries, I do not think you will have much doubt. When you consider how she had been left on the morning of the 12th March, and in what state she was found when the servants came back to the house ten days later, there can be no doubt that her injuries were the consequence of a quarrel with her husband, and were inflicted by him.

The third question is an important one for your consideration. Do you believe that the habits of this unfortunate woman have largely contributed to her death, and, but for her habits, that these injuries never would have led to that result?

Although that consideration does not necessarily prevent the crime coming under the category of murder, or take away from the prisoner his responsibility for his actions. However, it might weigh a good deal in your minds to reducing the offence from that of murder to that of culpable homicide.

The case is undoubtedly of the gravest nature. Anything more unmanly, more cowardly, more base, than that which has been shown here, whatever might be the name you should give it, could scarcely be conceived. I ask that you now consider your verdict.

The jury duly retired at ten minutes to seven o'clock, and the courtroom fell into a hushed silence of anticipation. Alexander Macdougall was led back to his dingy cell to await the verdict.

After an absence of just seventeen minutes, the jury returned.

Members of the jury, have you reached a verdict on which you all agree?

We have, your honour. We find the defendant guilty of culpable homicide.

Culpable homicide, like the verdict of 'not proven', is a peculiarly Scottish one enabling the jury to find some middle ground between murder and accidental death. The offence is defined under Scots law as causing the death of another person without planning or intending to, but through reckless behaviour. It differs to accidental death, in that there is clear criminal intention. It seems that Alexander Macdougall's boast to the police when first arrested, in which he claimed that no good Scottish jury would ever hang him, proved to be a correct one.

Lord Moncrieff, in passing sentence, addressed the prisoner directly, *The jury have dealt very mercifully with you. The sentence of the Court is that you be detained in penal servitude for ten years. Take him away.*

Alexander Macdougall shouted out his innocence as he was unceremoniously marched away, *It was not me, it was the drink!*

Prior to the trial, King's House Hotel had been sold to cover Macdougall's legal costs, which had amounted to more than £200. Happily, under new management, the hotel's fortunes dramatically improved. When Alexander

Wilkie MP visited in 1900, the tragic events of only 23 years earlier had been long forgotten:

Arriving at Kings House Inn to a hearty welcome. Tea, my clothes, and shoes dried. Next morning after a walk, I go in for breakfast. What shall I have? – grapefruit? What! Can I have grapefruit in Kings House; of course I can; and so I have grapefruit, and porridge and cream, and fish, and everything just like a West End city hotel. I am well looked after and at a charge so moderate that I am almost ashamed of my appetite.

Alexander Macdougall was eventually transferred to Murthly Lunatic Asylum in Perthshire, where he was recorded as an inmate on the '*General Register of Lunatics*' until 1890. He died in 1910.

The Macdougall's daughter, Elizabeth Christina, who had been sent away to live with relatives in Edinburgh as a young child, never saw her father or mother again. However, she did live a full life, eventually returning to live in Highland Perthshire (her mother and father's birthplace), before passing away in Aberfeldy in 1945 at the age of 73.

THE LOST JACOBITE GOLD
– THE HUNT CONTINUES

The chapter entitled *Lost Gold* in my previous book *Blood Beneath Ben Nevis* examined the ongoing search, and the legend surrounding, Prince Charles Edward Stuart's war chest, Bonnie Prince Charlie's legendary lost Jacobite gold. The total financial value of the missing treasure today might be in the order of £10 million; its historical significance to Scottish history is certainly incalculable.

Since the publication of that story, the hunt for the treasure continues unabated. There have been new and interesting discoveries, some disappointments, and some revelations. I received scores of messages from amateur gold-seekers, who, stirred by the story, had journeyed, or planned to travel, to the shores of Loch Arkaig. During the intervening years I, too, have sought further clues.

According to legend, the Spanish (alongside the French, both very much enemies of the English Government at the time) pledged to deliver a consignment of 400,000 Louis d'or gold coins every month to help bolster the Jacobite cause. Minted in 1745 by Louis XV of France, each coin was a flawless 24 carats. Due to the excellent minting techniques employed at the time, not only were the coins virtually impossible to forge, they were also happily accepted as an international trading currency.

Unfortunately, transporting the coins in bulk to the Jacobite army was an operation fraught with danger. The initial installment (sent via Charles's brother Henry who was resident in France at the time) was dispatched in 1745. This was followed, on 25th March 1746, by a French ship especially re-named *Le Prince Charles*, formerly the *HMS Hazard*, which carried £13,000 in gold, arms, and other supplies to Inverness. Regrettably, for Prince Charles Stuart, the ship was forced into the Kyle of Tongue in the far north of Scotland, while being pursued by the British frigate *HMS Sheerness*. During the night, the crew and soldiers on board *HMS Hazard* disembarked carrying the money. However, the following morning Captain George Mackay, son of the chief of the Clan Mackay, who supported the British government and King George II, confronted them at Druim na coub, and captured the shipment on behalf of the British. Despite this setback, and true to their word, the Spanish again attempted to send financial support to Bonnie Prince Charlie. On 30th April 1746 seven casks of gold coins, containing 1,200,000 French and Spanish gold coins, were landed on the west coast of Scotland by two French frigates, the *Bellona* and *Mars*. Unfortunately, the French crew on board the two vessels had not yet heard of Prince Charlie's defeat at the Battle of Culloden two weeks previously. As the French ships landed, they were spotted by British Navy frigates; and they hastily unloaded their cargo, enabling them to head back out into open waters and confront the incoming warships. After some intense fighting, the French vessels were able to inflict enough damage on one of the British warships to facilitate their escape back to France, leaving the precious cargo of gold coins behind.

With the Jacobite cause in disarray, the footsoldiers scattered across the Highlands, and Prince Charles and his loyal lieutenants in hiding, it was decided that the money should be used to assist the escape of Prince Charles and his trustworthy Jacobite clansmen across the channel to France. With a price on the prince's head, and with the Highland population subject to the punitive brutalities of the Duke of Cumberland's Redcoat army, it became vital that the Jacobite treasure did not fall into English hands.

Six caskets (one having already been stolen by McDonald of Barrisdale's men) were carried inland for 20 miles to Loch Arkaig and temporarily hidden. Their secret was entrusted to Murray of Broughton, one of the Jacobite fugitives. Murray then began the distribution of the gold coins to clan chiefs. Meanwhile, the Duke of Cumberland ordered 1,700 government troops, under the Earl of Loudon, into Lochaber to quell any attempt at an uprising. Murray of Broughton was apprehended by the British government (and turned state's evidence in exchange for his life). This forced the remaining Jacobite leaders to entrust the treasure, first to Lochiel, the chief of Clan Cameron, and then to Euan Macpherson of Cluny, head of Clan Macpherson.

The few precious clues to the location of this vast hoard have fascinated historians and treasure hunters alike for almost three centuries. Seemingly, the failure to locate the missing coins has fuelled, rather than dampened, their enthusiasm. I have spent the years since the publication of *Blood Beneath Ben Nevis* continuing my hunt for vital clues in the quest for the enigmatic prize. My search, it transpires, has been far from fruitless.

During February of 1898, Gilbert Heathcote-Drummond-Willoughby, the Earl of Ancaster, had undertaken some renovations in the east wing of the family's ancestral home, Drummond Castle, near Crieff in Perthshire, along the ancient cattle droving routes, and some 80 miles away from Lochaber.

The east wing, the oldest portion of the castle, was erected in the fifteenth century. While the Earl's joiners were stripping out the woodwork on the top floor, they discovered two coins carefully wrapped in paper and concealed above an old door frame. One of the coins was a silver double florin, bearing the inscription 'Jacobas II, Dei Gratia' (James II by the grace of God). And on the reverse side '1686. Mag. Br. Fra. et Hib. Rex.' (King of Great Britain, France, and Ireland). On the edge of the coin were etched the words, Decus et Putamen Anno Regni Secundo' (an ornament and a safeguard for the second year of your reign).

The second coin was a gold 'louis d'or', similar to those from the lost Jacobite hoard, and bearing the following inscription, 'Lud. XIII. D.G. Fr. Et Nav. Rex. 1702' (Louis

XIII, by the grace of God, King of France and Navarre).
On the reverse side was marked, 'Regn. Vine. Imp. Chrs.
(Christ reigns conquers and commands).

The workmen also uncovered a small hiding hole (known
as a 'bole') which had been covered with lath and plaster.
The secret bole had remained undetected for almost
two centuries; and was dated by experts to have been
constructed around the turn of the eighteenth century.

At the time mentioned on the first coin, 1686, James
Drummond, the fourth Earl of Perth was an ardent Jacobite
supporter and had been rewarded for his loyalty to the
cause. Following his death he was succeeded in title by his
son (also named James), who served in the 1715 rebellion.

The bloodline's loyalty to the Jacobite cause continued
with the fourth Earl's sons (James and John). James, the
third Duke, met Bonnie Prince at Culloden, but died just
two weeks after the shipment of gold coins had arrived on
the west coast of Scotland. He had managed to escape the
carnage at Culloden and reach the French ship *Bellona* in
the hope of reaching the continent. However, he died of
a fever on board and was buried at sea. If he did agree to
hide either the coins, or the prince, in a secret hiding place
at Drummond Castle, that information died along with the
duke.

His younger brother, John, became the fourth Duke of
Perth but he was killed in 1747 at the siege of Bergen
op Zoom in Belgium. John had also met the prince at
Culloden and escaped to France on the *Bellona* with his
brother. On his arrival in France, he became the first

Jacobite officer to give a first-hand account of the Battle of Culloden to the French Court at Versailles.

If the loyal Drummonds were indeed rewarded for supporting the Jacobite cause in 1686 and 1702, and fought in the rebellions of 1715 and 1745, then it seems a distinct possibility that they may have been entrusted to hide some of the 1746 shipment.

Conceivably, the two coins discovered were part of a larger consignment. Possibly, they were placed there in haste during a government search of the premises. They may also have been placed above the doorway as a good luck charm for all Jacobite supporters who unknowingly passed under them. This was a fairly common practice and believed to bring good fortune or protect against witchcraft.

Perhaps the estate at Drummond Castle may still contain another secret hoard of Jacobite coins, transported there by Prince Charles Stuart's supporters, following the arrival of the shipment from the continent. However, the castle was confiscated in punishment by the British government in 1750, conceivably meaning that a stash of lost Jacobite gold may have been concealed right under the noses of the Redcoat army. Or, in the case of the coins placed above the doorway, right over their heads.

It would also suggest that the search for the lost Jacobite gold might require the casting of a much wider net. The potential of locations further afield, such as Drummond Castle, may also explain the failure so far to locate the majority of the treasure in and around Loch Arkaig.

In 1931 it was reported that a small team of amateur
historians and archaeologists from Yorkshire had made a
study of the legend surrounding the missing Jacobite gold,
combined with an overlaid study of an early Ordnance
Survey map of Loch Arkaig (compiled between 1872 and
1878). The group became convinced that the weight of
evidence still pointed to:

*The fate of treasure being pretty well known. We are now certain
it was hidden close to the shores at the head of Loch Arkaig, and
buried in the bed of one of the streams which runs out into the loch.
We know that, by not one penny did the Prince benefit from the
'louis d'or' collected for him in France. Indeed, after years the Loch
Arkaig gold came to looked on by the Jacobites as more of curse than
anything else. We consider that the few who knew the whereabouts
of the gold failed to avail themselves of their knowledge, which
leaves us to suppose there is little doubt it is still there.*

The River Pean flows into Loch Arkaig at its head, and the
group were satisfied that the remote location, combined
with the steep grassy slopes in the area, meant that it may
not yet have been thoroughly searched. It was considered
that the sheer number of tributaries that flow from the
surrounding hillsides into the river, and the constantly
changing water level, would have ensured that the prince's
followers buried the coins close to a recognisable or
characteristic landmark, thus enabling them to return and
locate the treasure without difficulty. The early Ordnance
Survey map provided them with a detailed topography of
the river and its banks, helping them to highlight several
areas of potential interest. Their attention was drawn to
the small islands or outcrops of rocks that appeared within

the river when the water levels were low, but which were largely invisible when the river was swollen. Interestingly, two of these islands did appear on the 1878 Ordnance Survey map, but do not currently appear on Google maps (perhaps suggesting that the water level is higher now than 150 years ago, as it is in the loch itself). Alternatively, the flowing motion of the water may have eroded the rocky features to the extent that they no longer appear above the water's surface.

The group were also particularly fascinated by an indication on the earlier map of a series of stone steps across the River Dessary, which flows into the Pean at the tiny settlement of Strathan. These steps could have been used as a marker by any returning Jacobite followers planning on collecting the stash. Today, Strathan is a one-house community. Interestingly, however, close to this spot sits the ruins of Tigh nan Saighdearan, a small army barracks built by government forces shortly after the gold was reputedly hidden. The presence of these barracks seems to indicate two important points. Firstly, that after the consignment was brought across the Glenfinnan pass to Loch Arkaig, an informer may have given this information to the British government, leading them to station a number of soldiers at Tigh nan Saighdearan, in the hope of capturing the gold. And, secondly, that the presence of these soldiers may have discouraged any follower of Prince Charles Stuart returning to claim the gold, for fear of capture. This very important second point convinced the 1931 team from Yorkshire that the gold might still be within their grasp.

The group made a study of the *Bathymetrical Survey of Freshwater Lochs* (compiled between 1897-1909), which recorded in detail the depths in every part of Loch Arkaig, as well as highlighting surrounding footpaths and features of interest in the River Pean. Coupled with two recently discovered letters, the team carefully plotted their intended search area.

The first letter, from Murray of Broughton the Prince's secretary, detailed an account of the treasure's distribution:

Six casks of French gold landed at Burradale containing Louis-d'ors, £35,000. On the discharge side appears the following: The sum of 15,000 Louis-d'ors, 1,000 in each bag, counted over exactly, it was then divided into three parcels, 5,000 in each; one parcel was put under a rock in a small rivulet, the other two parcels in the ground at a little distance, the holes made, and the money deposited by Sir Stewart Thriepland, Mr Alexander MacLeod, Major Kennedy, and Dr Cameron.

Sir Stewart Thriepland's account of the events also seems to confirm this:

Buried near to the head of Lochakaig, opposite to Callich, Louis-d'ores, £15,000. Twelve thousand pounds was buried near the foot of the lake. This money was buried in two parcels, 6,000 in each, all in bags of 1,000 each. The night before we were obliged to retire from Lochiel's house of Achnacarry, Doctor Cameron and Mr Alexander MacLeod, carried it upon their shoulders from the above-mentioned house.

The team from Yorkshire also took particular interest in a letter penned in Lille, in France, by James Edgar (the

former secretary to King James III) to Prince Charles
Stuart's private secretary in 1753:

*I wish with all my heart that the Government had got it all at the
beginning, for it has given the greatest stroke to the cause that can
be imagined. It has divided the different clans more than ever. The
money proved a curse to all concerned until Cluny bore all he could
back to France.*

The letter clearly implies that, although some of the
gold seems to have been spirited away to France; at least
some of the treasure remained unclaimed (this would be
proved almost a century later and is dealt with later in this
chapter).

Armed with this information, the Yorkshire team made
a search of possible locations around the head of Loch
Arkaig during the late summer of 1931. Sadly, their
endeavours proved fruitless. Finally, as the weather
worsened and their funding dried up, the pursuit was
abandoned. The failure of their search, however, was
deemed to be due to the team's underestimation of the
difficulty of the terrain and task at hand, rather than their
initial assumptions.

Inspired by the challenge, several amateur explorers and
treasure hunters returned to the Loch during the following
summer and continued the search. One man, a Highland
minister, on his summer break, was fishing from a rowing
boat near the shore of Loch Arkaig when he hooked
something unusually heavy. With his ghillie's help they
reeled in their catch which suddenly and mysteriously
seemed to be much lighter than they had at first thought.

The ghillie immediately exclaimed to the minister, 'It's one o' the Prince's money bags. I know it!', however the find slipped agonisingly from their line. Convinced they had located a portion of the lost treasure they tried in vain to re-hook the mysterious and heavy object, but without luck. Their day was not without success however - they did manage to snare a 15-pound salmon!

Interest in the hunt for the prince's treasure waned with the approach of the Second World War and it was not until online digital archiving, and improvements in technology allowing for the production of lighter and more portable metal detectors, that interest in the quest for the Jacobite gold was reawakened.

The hunt for the elusive treasure was about to enter an exciting new era.

THE LOST GOLD
– ANSWERS AND QUESTIONS

The disappointments and tantalising clues in the hunt for the lost Jacobite gold would finally lead to a degree of resolution as the twenty-first century arrived. Yet, as ever, in the pursuit of this legendary treasure, every answer seemed to raise yet another question.

Nevertheless, one team of intrepid explorers believed that the answer to the location of Bonnie Prince Charlie's lost gold lay somewhere else entirely. Their research led them to believe there was another unmentioned, and as yet undiscovered, hoard of gold destined for the Jacobite cause, that never actually reached the west coast of Scotland.

During the 1990s a diving expert, while exploring the seabed off the coast of Anglesey in North Wales at the possible sight of a shipwreck, uncovered a small copper disc which he initially dismissed as a worthless coin of little value or interest, and left it to languish in a drawer.

However, many years later, while discussing his find with a friend, he was encouraged to send the disc to be examined by numismatist experts at the National Museum of Scotland in Edinburgh. A microscopic study revealed that the surface of the disc featured an identical duplicate of the seal on the signet ring worn by Mary Queen of Scots at her execution. It was believed by the expedition's organiser that the seal had been used by the ship's captain as a form of identification used to confirm the authenticity of the carrier; and to prove that the ship did not contain British spies sent to track down the prince.

This led a 20-strong dive team to re-explore the site, under the assumption that the seabed might contain the wreckage of a French or Spanish galleon sent by Louis XV, to finance the Jacobite rebellion. Operations began well, organised dives were undertaken to explore the site and a flight of scaffolding was erected down the rugged cliff face for easy access. £70,000 of investment was raised to finance the project and arrangements were made for the filming of a television documentary to record the historic find. It was hoped to find the remainder of the vessel's bell to identify the ship's name and thus any record of its voyage. The leader of the dive team was convinced that the galleon had been sent with a further consignment of gold coins to help finance the prince's escape from the Isle of Skye following the disastrous defeat at Culloden (see the earlier chapter *The Prince Over the Water*).

However, by September 2009, the operation had run into financial difficulties and further money was sought from investors. By 2010 the ill-fated project had stalled completely, and the worried financial backers sought a return of their investment, doubting the authenticity of the original project.

Eventually, all exploration ground to a halt and, sadly, no gold was ever recovered. The real reason for the presence of Mary Queen of Scot's seal on the seabed off the coast of Anglesey remains a mystery.

However, the anti-climax of the 2009 seabed search did not curtail the enthusiasm of those dedicated to solving the mystery. A Discovery Channel programme, part of the *Expedition Unknown* series, together with the release of *Blood Beneath Ben Nevis* helped bring the story to the fore again in 2020. Immediately following publication of the book, two more important discoveries have also helped us to further understand, the mystery surrounding the lost Jacobite gold.

In 2020 a group of dedicated Scottish amateur archaeologists and historical researchers, known as 'Conflicts of Interest', was given permission to metal detect near a ruined croft house once owned by the Prince's Gaelic tutor, Alastair MacDonald. The group, knowing that the supplies destined for the Prince had been landed at Loch nan Uamh, then split into several separate packages and transported inland, were able to narrow down their field of search. This enabled the team to make a startling discovery. Buried close to the abandoned croft, the team unearthed a hoard of 215 Jacobite musket balls, gilt buttons, and coins. The find was immediately reported to the Treasure Trove unit at the National Museum of Scotland. Although the find did not contain any of the fabled treasure, it did prove that the story of Jacobite-bound supplies being shipped from French and Spanish vessels to Loch nan Uamh, then distributed inland and buried, was factual and not merely legend. The discovery of the lost treasure seemed closer than it had done for many years.

However, the most remarkable discovery was yet to come when an antique silver cup, once belonging to Prince Charles Stuart, was auctioned at Doyle's Auction House in New York on 31st October 2018. The cup, bearing the innocuous description, *'Lot 252, George II Silver Covered Two Handle Cup'*, led author and historian Martyn Downer to unearth the answer to the question that has plagued researchers for generations.

During April 1748, two years after his defeat on the battlefield at Culloden, Prince Charles Stuart was penurious and threatened with expulsion from his enforced exile in France. Desperate, the Prince despatched a secret coded order to Ewan MacPherson of Cluny (chief of the Clan Macpherson, and his most loyal officer) requesting him to enlist the help of a Jacobite secret agent known as 'Thomas Newton', who was at that time serving with the French government. Newton was in fact Major Kennedy, an Irish officer who had been one of the prince's most trusted bodyguards at Culloden. Cluny and Kennedy were instructed by Prince Charles to recover the gold coins and transport them to London. From his hiding place at 'the cage' in the mountains of the Highlands, Cluny readily agreed to assist in whatever he could. Unfortunately, Major Kennedy was unable to return to Scotland for fear he would be captured by Redcoat forces.

Instead, Kennedy journeyed to Newcastle and recruited Northumbrian farmer Charles Selby from Earle, near Wooler in Northumberland. Charles Selby was thought to have known Major Kennedy through their mutual Jacobite freemasonry connections

Charles Selby's father William had been imprisoned by the British government following his participation in the earlier 1715 Jacobite rebellion and had died in 1723. His son Charles believed that his father's early death was due to the harsh treatment he had received whilst incarcerated by the British. This fact, no doubt, led to Charles Selby's fervent support for the Jacobite cause. When asked by Major Kennedy to assist in the recovery of the gold, Charles Selby seized his opportunity to serve the exiled Prince, telling Kennedy that:

I am sincerely yours to command at any time, & particularly when it is a question of anything that regards our Dear friend, whom I should always serve at the expense of my life & fortune.

Major Kennedy was then introduced to Cluny's brother-in-law, Donald Macpherson of Breachachie, with whom Charles Selby was also acquainted. Both Donald MacPherson and Cluny had been together on the shores of Loch nan Uamh on 19th September 1746 when Prince Charles finally escaped from Scotland to the Continent. Donald MacPherson agreed to recover the gold and carry it as far south as the Scottish border; at which point the hoard would be handed over to Charles Selby. Selby then planned to hide the gold at his Northumbrian farmhouse, until he received instructions from the Prince. In a chain of

secret correspondence between the two men, in which the
rendezvous was arranged, Donald MacPherson was referred
to only as 'D'._

Once safely in Northumberland, Charles Selby, together
with his trusted (and heavily armed) servant, transported
the gold coins south to London in two separate trips.
With the threat of capture from government forces, or the
armed highwaymen that often lay waiting menacingly in
the shadows alongside England's roads, the trek south must
have been fraught with worry.

Thankfully the journeys passed without incident and the
coins were distributed to various trusted, but clandestine,
Jacobite bankers. The money was then converted to notes
and sent across the channel to the prince. In this way
some £6,000 was recovered from under the noses of the
authorities and shipped to France.

Charles Selby refused the offer of a reward from the
prince, in return for the risk he had taken. However, Prince
Charles insisted on recognising Selby's courage in risking
his own life and set upon the idea of presenting him with
a token of his appreciation instead. In keeping with the
other aristocrats of the time, the prince enjoyed displaying
as many symbols of wealth and trappings of his status as was
possible. Silver cups were considered to hold the highest
status among all silver objects. They were both practical
and prized and could be used in ceremonies and given as
courtly tokens of appreciation or for diplomatic exchanges.

Prince Charles chose a particularly fine cup as a gift for
Charles Selby. The cup had been made in 1743 by a highly

regarded London silversmith named Paul Crespin. It was approximately ten inches high, with two leaf-capped handles, a pedestal base, and a domed cover. The cup had been embellished with various symbols of Jacobite sovereignty and re-birth, such as roses and flowers. The cup was of great significance as it closely resembled a similar cup which had been among the prince's canteen captured during the defeat at Culloden.

On the reverse of the trophy a cartouche bearing an inscription was added at a later stage, which read as follows:

> *From Prince Charles Edwd Stuart*
> *To Chas Selby Esqr of Earle*
> *in Remembrance of His Many Services*
> *in 1745 & 1746*

It seems most likely that the inscription was engraved onto the silver cup at some point towards the end of the eighteenth century, probably by Charles Selby's son, Thomas Selby. The award of the silver cup, and Charles Selby's part in smuggling the illicit Jacobite gold to France, was kept a closely guarded secret during his lifetime. Had he been caught in the act by the English authorities, he would undoubtedly have faced public execution. Charles Selby made no mention of the silver cup in his will, nor did he discuss it publicly during his lifetime. He did, however, go to the extraordinary risk of having a portrait painted in which he is shown proudly displaying the cup.

Over the following two centuries the cup and portrait became separated, and the secret forgotten, until the portrait was found in Edinburgh during the 1970s and the silver cup resurfaced at the New York auction in 2018. Martyn Downer was able to trace the provenance of the painting through a descendent of Charles Selby and, after some lengthy research, finally put the pieces of the puzzle together.

This interesting breakthrough does provide us with some resolution to the saga; and a final destination for approximately 40% of the lost Jacobite treasure. However, the search for the remaining £9,000 supposedly buried near Loch Arkaig, which may have been stolen or scattered across many locations, is still far from being resolved.

In addition to that possibility, is an often forgotten and potentially enticing prospect, that yet more shipments of gold were sent to assist other loyal Jacobites still in hiding, long after the Prince had finally escaped to France on the 20th September 1746.

While researching this chapter, I uncovered an interesting newspaper article from more than a century ago. In early 1900 an interesting and extremely old letter was unearthed in Dingwall, north of Inverness, and the find reported in a newspaper article dated March 1900. The letter highlighted some of the problems that the arrival of such large amounts of money in the Highlands caused. The newspaper article told of a portmanteau containing:

a few thousand pounds in gold which was landed at Coigach (a peninsula north of Ullapool) *for distribution among the prince's adherents; but 'busy bodies' were soon at work. Large rewards were offered to entice any information to the location of the money.*

The final resting place of this particular consignment of coins is still unaccounted for. It appeared that two officers working for the British Government, but claiming to be loyal to Bonnie Prince Charlie, seized the shipment from loyal Jacobites.

The anonymous letter, reputed to have been written by a loyal Mackenzie, lamented the 'sorry features of the '45, and the prince's accursed gold, which led to imputations which survive to this day.' The letter relating the story reads as follows:

Saturday last, Alexander Mackenzie of Lentran and John Mackenzie of Torridon, two rebel officers of Lord Cromertie's Regiment, came to this place with a party of men to the number of 16 or 17, armed with guns, swords, and pistols, and forcibly carried away Murdoch Mackenzie, another of the officers of Lord Cromertie's Regt., and marched with him to the hill above Dingwall. It is said that the reason for apprehending Murdoch is that he might deliver up to these gentleman officers some money which he had in his custody, that was landed at Coigach, a port on Lord Cromertie's estate in the Highlands.

The ship came to the Highlands some time after the battle of Culloden, and delivered a portmanteau containing £3,000 sterling and upwards (worth upwards of £700,000 today), *to Major William Mackenzie, brother to the Laird of Kilcoy Castle, and to*

Colin Mackenzie, alias Roy, brother to Dundonald, and to the above Murdoch Mackenzie.

The King's troops, being then in the country close by, the three men divided the money for their own private use. But is now given out that there is an order from the Pretender requiring these men to deliver up the money to the gentleman who still adhere to his interest in this country. What greater contempt of Government than to pretend to come by legal authority from the Pretender to a royal burgh within six or seven miles of the garrison of Inverness!

D M R, Dingwall, 10ᵗʰ March, 1747

Although a large proportion of the 1746 shipment can now be accounted for, thanks to the work of Martyn Downer, there may still be a substantial cache of gold coins buried somewhere – probably split across multiple locations – and lying undisturbed, well-hidden, and waiting to be unearthed. Indeed, the 1747 letter above hints at further shipments which may yet lie undiscovered. Every year Scottish historians seem to edge agonisingly closer to solving this most elusive and romantic of mysteries.

Perhaps, the story of the lost Jacobite gold may yet have more secrets to reveal.

* * * * * *

For those who wish to read more about the hunt for the lost Jacobite gold, please refer to the chapter *Lost Gold*, in *Blood Beneath Ben Nevis*.

Anyone wishing to undertake their own search for missing treasure should remember the difficulty and remoteness of the terrain surrounding some of the possible locations of the gold and be adequately prepared.

Please also respect the unspoilt nature of these regions and leave each area as you originally found it. If you do locate any object that might be of interest, you must report your find to the Treasure Trove Unit at the National Museum of Scotland, or to your local council's archaeological finds officer.

THE LOCH LINNHE MURDER
(PART ONE)

Loch Linnhe lies on the line of the Great Glen fault, approximately 30 miles in length from the Firth of Lorne in the southwest to the mouth of the River Lochy at Fort William in the northeast. Despite its stunning beauty and the splendour of the surroundings, the great sea loch, which derives its name from the Gaelic word *linne*, meaning 'pool', has witnessed many maritime mysteries and tragically lost lives.

Loch Linnhe holds a number of secrets too. From the boy who ran home to his mother at Corran in 1866, telling of 'a

ghost floatin down the loch on nothin at all', to the farmer who fished a bottle from the loch, near Fort William, in 1866 containing the note, 'Lost at sea, the ship 'Eagle', lat.65 North – 48 West. No hope now. Ship sinking; evening of 23 April 1865.' The coordinates referred to a location close to the Arctic Russian port of Archangelsk. How did a bottle from the frozen Barents Sea drift thousands of miles into a Scottish sea loch?

Initially, there seemed to be no great mystery about the murder committed aboard the fishing smack *Heather Bell* in Loch Linnhe on the night of the 25th of June 1874. However, the actual course of events would transpire to be very different indeed.

The *Heather Bell*, part of the Buckie fishing fleet from the east coast of Scotland, was returning from a herring catch just off the coast of the Knock peninsula in the Western Isles. The crew of four intended to return home to Banff via Loch Linnhe and the Caledonian Canal. The trip had been a bountiful one and the vessel was well stocked with barrels of herring. Newly built in Macduff, this was the maiden voyage for the half-decked lugger. Supposedly built for a crew of five, on this voyage the smack was operating with only four members of crew, the additional space being required for a pony which was needed to pull the boat through the locks on the Caledonian Canal. The crew consisted of William Scott, the part owner of the *Heather Bell* and the self-appointed skipper, his son James, William MacDonald, and James Smith. William Scott was the eldest, at 52, and considered himself the ablest sailor. His son James was 21. James Smith was 25, a fisherman from

Macduff with a violent temper and a scowling complexion. William MacDonald was the junior crew member, quieter than the other men and placed in charge of the pony.

After successfully catching their quota the crew of the *Heather Bell* began their return journey. They stopped at Tobermory on the Isle of Mull for provisions, feed for the pony, and, crucially, to purchase whisky for the return voyage. According to a witness in the town, 'the men indulged rather freely in liquor in the harbour and carried away with them a large supply of it.'

The *Heather Bell* sailed away from Tobermory around 5pm on the 25th June 1874. It was a sunny and pleasant evening at the height of summer and the waters were calm. As the vessel navigated its way through the Sound of Mull, past Duart Castle, and into Loch Linnhe it became clear all was not well aboard. James Smith was at the helm and drinking heavily. His temper had already been inflamed by William Scott, who had refused to reboard the boat at Tobermory when Smith had requested him to. It seemed that William Scott, as the senior crew member and part owner of the fishing smack, took exception to receiving orders from James Smith. The two younger men, James Scott and William MacDonald, although having also imbibed rather too freely, were manning the sails and maintaining a lookout. William Scott disapproved wholeheartedly of the younger men's drunken behaviour and admonished them openly. He particularly singled out James Smith and shouted his objections to Smith's steering of the vessel and his general inability to keep the wake arrow straight.

'I will steer the *Heather Bell*,' said William Scott, 'she is my ship!'

Smith retaliated furiously, claiming, 'I am the best sailor aboard, old man, you will take the helm when I say so, and not before.'

The unpleasantness continued as the crew entered Loch Linnhe, fuelled by copious amounts of whisky. James Smith, it appears, then had a sudden change of heart and turned to William Scott, saying, 'I am tired and need to go to my rest. You take the helm now, old man.'

William Scott refused, claiming that he was also too tired. Around 10pm, and sensing yet another argument brewing between James Smith and his father, James Scott informed everyone that he was going to the forecastle to sleep off the whisky. He stumbled below deck into the forward part of the boat and quickly fell into a deep slumber.

The following morning James Scott woke up still very much the worse for wear and, after rubbing his eyes, staggered out onto the deck. To his surprise the *Heather Bell* was close to the shoreline near Fort William. Looking around, he noticed young William MacDonald busying himself on the deck. The vessel seemed to be drifting aimlessly, the helm was unmanned. Neither his father nor James Smith were anywhere to be seen.

James Scott enquired, 'William, where's my father?'

William MacDonald replied, but his answers were vague and evasive, 'He might have gone back to Tobermory, or maybe got off.'

Next, he asked James Smith, who had been below decks, 'Where's my father?'

Again, Smith's answer was ambiguous and seemed improbable, 'He went back to Tobermory and maybe got another boat there. He said he would join you in Corpach.' (a village close to the entrance to the Caledonian Canal)

James Scott was unsurprisingly troubled by the pair's vague responses, 'How did he get back? Why didn't you wake me?'

This time William MacDonald answered, 'I tried to rouse you, but you would not move.'

When they reached Corpach, James Scott disembarked while Smith and MacDonald remained onboard the *Heather Bell.* There were a small number of fishing vessels moored there, some of which were known to James Scott, and he quickly ran from boat to boat enquiring if any of the other fishermen had seen his father. However, his efforts were futile. No one had seen or heard from William Scott since the crew of the *Heather Bell* had been seen drinking together in Tobermory during the previous afternoon. James Scott returned immediately to his own boat. As he boarded his eyes were drawn to what appeared to be a bloodstained piece of cloth lying on the deck among the ropes. As he bent down to pick it up, he realised that the cloth was, in fact, a cravat or necktie, of a type often worn by fishermen. Scott instantly recognised the cravat. It was his father's. He turned to William MacDonald, this time more peremptorily, 'Where the hell is my father?'

MacDonald answered quietly, his head lowered, 'you will see your father no more.'

Scott's heart sank. He told MacDonald to wait where he was, and he yelled out to another fisherman loafing by the moorings, 'Fetch a Fort William policeman as quickly as you can!'

Soon afterwards, Constable Fraser, stationed at Corpach, together with a colleague from Fort William, Constable Macaskill, boarded the *Heather Bell*. Constable Fraser questioned William MacDonald, who explained that there had been a terrible accident onboard. Meanwhile, Constable Macaskill searched the boat. It did not take long to unearth some sinister clues in the puzzling disappearance of William Scott. In addition to the bloodstained cravat, there were tell-tale signs of blood on the wooden rails, on parts of the decking, on a chest, and on one of the herring barrels. With this potentially crucial evidence and the reticent behaviour of the two men, it was decided to detain them for questioning. James Smith and William MacDonald were then taken to Fort William police station and interrogated.

The two men were questioned separately. James Smith remained tight-lipped and uncommunicative, and seemed to the officers to have a furtive and guilty demeanour. Despite being pressed heavily during his interrogation, Smith refused to answer any questions, other than to claim complete bewilderment in the disappearance of William Scott. William MacDonald, on the other hand, was terrified and anxious to explain everything to the officers. A statement was written down on his behalf and MacDonald signed it with a scrawled mark (he was unable to read or write):

I was stationed in the boat as lookout, and old Scott steered. James Smith, the other man in custody, sat behind me. Nothing of an unpleasant nature occurred while we were running down the Sound of the Mull until about ten o'clock, when, on entering into Linnhe Loch, Smith wished old Scott to take over the helm and allow him to steer, as he needed his rest. Scott refused, and they had angry words. Smith tried to grab old Scott and, in the struggle, Smith struck him a severe blow on the forehead, which caused his blood to flow. In the excitement, passion seized Smith and he grabbed old Scott by both his legs, and he threw him overboard, using at the time the expression, "Let the devil go to the bottom!" This happened so quickly that before I could interpose old Scott was under the water. I endeavoured to rouse his son young Scott, but could not, and afterwards the boat was allowed to drift on at random. This state of matters continued until the next morning, when young Scott, having awakened, missed his father. He enquired about his father but he only received evasive answers from me and James Smith, so he called the police.

The well-crafted statement was damning evidence indeed. James Smith was immediately charged by the Fort William police with the murder of William Scott; to which he pleaded 'I am not guilty'. He was then removed to Inverary Jail to await trial. William MacDonald was released without charge by the police, despite having some bloodstaining upon his clothing, and allowed to return to the *Heather Bell*.

The two remaining crew members, James Scott and William MacDonald, re-joined the Buckie fishing fleet and continued their onward journey along the 60 miles of the Caledonian Canal towards home. However, it would not be long until further tragedy struck. At the Banavie Locks (known as Neptune's Staircase) a fisherman on another vessel slipped and fell from his boat into the dark waters of the canal. The powerful reflux of the water crushed his body between the hull and the side of the lock. Despite efforts from James Scott and several other fishermen, who managed to haul the unfortunate man from the water, he passed away shortly afterwards from his catastrophic injuries. It was a salutary lesson that, even away from the open seas and in the comparative safety of the canal, working conditions for fishermen were frequently fraught with danger.

Meanwhile, James Smith remained incarcerated while the Fort William police began their investigation. It was soon discovered that James Smith had a reputation for heavy drinking and had been jailed twice before. Once for a violent altercation in Banff, for which he received six-month's penal servitude (hard labour) in Banff Jail. He previously also used the alias 'Alexander Johnston' while housebreaking and had received a second prison sentence for theft. However, despite these damning revelations, Smith continued to protest his innocence. His trial date was set for Thursday 1st October 1874.

As Lord George Young opened the proceedings at the Inverary Court House on that Thursday morning in 1874, there was a general feeling that the country had entered a new era of enlightenment and understanding. The first general election held under a secret ballot had recently taken place, as Britain's system of democracy gradually ground its way towards that which is recognisable today. The newly passed *Factory Act 1874* had limited the working week to just 56 hours; raised the minimum working age to nine; and banned the use of children as chimney sweeps.

The generally positive feeling extended into the Inverary courtroom that morning. Lord Young was a popular, progressive judge and Liberal politician who had famously introduced the *Education Act* in Scotland during 1872, ensuring free schooling for all children in the country. He immediately pardoned the first prisoner of the day, a man named John Duncan, who had previously escaped from Inverary Jail. Lord Young felt that Duncan's incarceration on remand had been unacceptably long. On hearing this news, James Smith's heart leapt with joy. Despite having continually pleaded his innocence in the murder of William Scott, he had been imprisoned for three months while awaiting trial. However, he was to receive no such pretrial pardon, as he was escorted into the dock by two prison guards. The trial commenced:

James Smith, fisherman and native of MacDuff, you are hereby charged that on the night of 25th June, or the morning of the 26th June last, that you throw overboard and did murder William Scott, a Banffshire fisherman, and did dispose of his body into the Sound of Mull in an attempt to conceal your crime. How do you plead?

Not guilty, your Lordship.

Very well. We shall proceed. Mr Gloag, please proceed for the Crown in this matter.

The prosecution, led by Mr William Gloag QC, called their first witness, William MacDonald.

Mr MacDonald, you served as mate onboard the Heather Bell, is that correct?

Yes sir. The crew consisted of myself, the deceased, Mr William Scott, his son James, and the prisoner James Scott.

Thank you, please explain to the court what happened on the 25th June last.

We reached Tobermory about midday, intending to go through the Caledonian Canal. They went ashore to get some provender (animal fodder) *for the pony we had on board, and some whisky for themselves.*

Did you remain on board?

Yes sir.

Very well, please proceed.

There was some quarrelling amongst them when they returned to the boat, which Smith and young Scott began. First young Scott, then his father, would not get back on board when Smith wanted them to. But after a while Smith took hold of old Scott by the arms, and went on board with him. That was about five or six in the afternoon. As James Scott was a good deal worse of drink, he went below to his bed.

William Scott was steering, Smith and I were working at the sails. After the Point of Strangers (Tobermory Lighthouse), *near the island of Calve, about three miles or so off Tobermory, a strife took place between Smith and old Scott about the steering of the boat. Smith wanted old Scott to give him the helm, which Scott refused to do. Smith struck him on the face with his closed fist and the blood sprang. I cried out, 'God preserve us, men. what's this?'*

Before I could do anything, Smith took old Scott by the shoulders and legs and threw him over the quarter deck of the boat into the sea, saying 'Let the old devil go to the bottom'.

And did have a clear view of this whole affair, Mr MacDonald? Mr Gloag enquired.

It was not yet dark, but I did not notice whether he went backwards or face foremost. I ran down into the hold, and tried to rouse young Scott, pulling him by the legs, and shouting to him, but he was so dead drunk that he couldn't move. Just before going under the deck I saw old Scott floating away astern. His body was still there when I came up again. I let go of the sails and tried to turn the boat, but I couldn't do anything to save him. When I looked round again after trying to turn the boat, he was gone out of sight, lost in our cutwater, sir.

And what did the accused do during this time, Mr MacDonald?

Smith did nothing and said nothing on deck, sir, then he went below deck immediately after I came up from trying to rouse the son. Then, about a quarter of an hour later Smith came aft, from forward somewhere on the boat. I was steering then. He helped me to put up the sail again. Nothing was said between us at that time.

After some time Smith went below again, and I was alone on deck till daybreak. I sat down on the barrels and grat (an old Scots word for cried) *for a good while. No one was steering then. I felt bad about the old man being gone. Smith came up at daylight. He wanted to steer the boat. I gave him the helm and I said to him, 'surely we are going the wrong way now?' He said, 'She's going right enough. I don't care a damn if she goes to the bottom. When the thing is done it is done.' Then he* (Smith) *let go of the helm and went to bed, and he did not come back till eight in the morning.*

There were audible murmurs of disapproval from the

public gallery as the Crown continued their interrogation of the witness:

And tell the court please, Mr MacDonald, did you see or hear any other boats during all of this time?

I saw no boat then or at any time during the night. Although we might have been hailed outwith my hearing. I might have been slumbering also.

Very well. Thank you. And what did the prisoner say to you when he arose in the morning?

Well, sir, when we were getting near the canal mouth Smith said to me, 'Do you have something on your mind? If you do, I'll get it out of you! You had better take care how you report this case to the police, or it will be banishment for you.

And what do you think he meant by this? asked Mr Gloag.

Well, sir, I took it to mean things would be very bad for me if I told folks what really happened.

Very well, please continue.

Yes, sir. When we got close to the dock, I told young Scott that his father was drowned in the Sound of Mull; I did not say whether by accident or not. When ashore I told the constable about the drowning. I then told the whole truth to the Procurator-Fiscal at Fort William.

The packed courtroom was then given a short recess before the defence barrister Mr Jameson was given the opportunity to cross-witness William MacDonald.

The case against James Smith appeared watertight. Would the defence be able to persuade the jury that even a scintilla of doubt existed in their client's guilt?

THE LOCH LINNHE MURDER
(PART TWO)

Following the recess, Mr Jameson began his defence of James Smith by cross-examining William MacDonald:

Tell the court, Mr MacDonald, what did you first say to the constable at Corpach harbour?

I may have tried to make him think that old Mr Scott fell overboard accidently. I don't remember exactly what I told the constable. MacDonald replied.

And yet you now claim that Mr Scott was thrown overboard by my client?

I made a statement to say that, yes.

Very well, let us move on. Where was my client when the police constables first came aboard the Heather Bell?

He was below deck.

And did my client come up on deck when the police boarded? enquired Mr Jameson.

He did, yes.

Please explain for the court what happened next.

Well, there were two barrels standing near the stern. One was full of water, and the other had herring in it. There was also a wooden chest there. Smith asked me if I knew how the blood came to be on them. Because the police were on board then, I said I did not know how the blood got there.

At this point in the cross-examination the judge, Lord Young, interjected with a question of his own:

Mr MacDonald, after what you have already told this court happened between the prisoner and William Scott, did it not appear odd to you that the prisoner should ask how the blood came to be there?

I did not think of that, responded William Macdonald.

Lord Young continued, *But it does appear odd; if what you said earlier was true when you stated that the prisoner grabbed Mr Scott's leg and threw him overboard. On the other hand, it would not be strange that Mr Smith did not know how the blood came to be there, if your earlier story to this court was false.*

Mr Jameson, for the defence, quickly seized on the judge's obvious dissatisfaction with William MacDonald's testimony and continued his cross-examination,

Mr MacDonald, was old Mr Scott the worse for drink?

Yes, he was, but I cannot tell you if he had any more drink after getting back on board at Tobermory.

Very well, Mr Jameson continued, *I put it to you that his death may have been nothing but an accident.*

William MacDonald did not answer. Unperturbed, Mr Jameson continued:

Was not old Mr Scott both taller and heavier than the prisoner? I am also taken to understand that he was stronger too. Would it not have been impossible for the smaller and weaker man to heave old Mr Scott overboard?

I don't know about that, sir.

And would not the gunwale of the boat have prevented Mr Scott from falling over the side? Surely it would catch him about halfway up the thigh?

I cannot answer that, sir.

And what about your deliberate misleading of Mr Scott's son, as to the whereabouts of his father?

William MacDonald's demeanour in the witness box now changed considerably. He seemed to appear somewhat confused as he continued his testimony, his answers stilted and nervous:

I have to say, sir, I am doubtful now of the exact words which I told to young Scott about his father's death. I think I told him that James Smith was on deck at the time. He did not ask me why I did not waken him, he only asked me why I had not done anything to save his father. That is all I can remember.

Again, this seemed to contradict the earlier statements made by MacDonald, in which he claimed to have misled James Scott regarding the events surrounding his father's disappearance. Finally, Lord Young's renowned patience reached its end. The witness's constant hesitations and contradictions were clearly compromising the trial. Taking his gavel in his hand, Lord Young addressed William MacDonald in the witness box:

Mr MacDonald, it appears to me that you could not possibly have done less than you did, or more determinedly left Mr Scott to perish, than if you had thrown him overboard to perish yourself.

William MacDonald seemed noticeably flustered by the judge's remarks and shuffled awkwardly in the witness box. Lord Young stared intently at him for a moment before announcing to the court, *Let the witness be removed.*

Lord Young then turned his attention to the prosecution counsel, Mr Gloag, and addressed him, *Mr Advocate-Depute, if you have no other evidence which is practically different from that which we have just heard, it is unnecessary to proceed further with this case.*

Mr Gloag's case for the prosecution had fallen to pieces in the courtroom, his key witness had proved unreliable, and the evidence given by him had been filled with inconsistencies and mistruths. In desperation he suggested to Lord Young that, *It might be advisable to examine the son of the deceased on several points of interest, your Honour.*

This was agreed to, and James Scott was called to the witness box. Lord Young insisted on questioning James Scott himself, enquiring, *Mr Scott, are you able to confirm any of the evidence given by the previous witness?*

However, James Scott was to prove of little help to the Crown's case. He contradicted William MacDonald's evidence in several material particulars, stating that, *the evidence of the first witness, regarding what passed between himself and James Smith, is untrue.*

And, Mr Scott, what of the evidence given by the first witness regarding your father's manner of death?

I wish to contradict that evidence, your Honour. There was no conversation in which we discussed the manner of my father's death. In fact, I overheard James Smith, when he was in MacDonald's presence, saying that he (Smith) *was below deck when this terrible thing happened to my father.*

And did Mr MacDonald disagree or dispute the prisoner's claim that he was below decks at the time of Mr Scott's death? Lord Young enquired.

No, your Honour, he accepted it without argument. He did not attempt to deny it.

William MacDonald had retaken his seat in the courtroom, and Lord Young glanced sternly at him before continuing his address, *Thank you Mr Scott, and do you wish to say anything else in this case which you feel may be of importance?*

Yes, your Honour. My father had a quarrel with MacDonald when we were off the Western Isles. MacDonald had been complaining to all of us about the quality of the cooking and the food onboard the boat. My father told me that he was tired of MacDonald complaining and would speak to him about this matter when the time was right.

On hearing this, Mr Gloag, on behalf of the Crown, withdrew the charge of murder. Lord Young then formally directed the jury to return a verdict of not guilty in the case of The Crown v James Smith. Lord Young then addressed James Smith, stating, *Mr Smith, the case against you has been dismissed. You are free to leave to courtroom without a stain on your character.*

James Smith was jubilant on hearing this news, and he turned to receive a cheer from the public gallery as he left Inverary Courthouse. Lord Young immediately suppressed the raucous behaviour, banging his gavel impatiently on the desk in front of him. He clearly did not wish his courtroom to descend any further into farce.

The mistrial verdict in the case brought against James Smith for the murder of William Scott left a rather bitter taste in the mouth of all those involved. Several important questions also remain unanswered.

Firstly, was William Scott actually murdered at all? Is it possible that his death was primarily the result of a fight between himself and either James Smith or William MacDonald, and not a premeditated murder? If just one witness had been able to testify to this effect, then a charge of culpable homicide may have been a reasonable and justifiable one to level against either (or both) men. Secondly, was William Scott's death merely a tragic accident, perhaps caused by an overindulgence in alcohol or a sudden rocking of the fishing boat? This seems the least plausible scenario; since Scott was an experienced fisherman and accustomed to the waters of Loch Linnhe. In addition, the gunwales of the *Heather Bell* would have afforded him some protection in the event of an unexpected fall. To the logical mind, it appears unlikely that a man might topple over the side of a boat, when his natural movement in suddenly losing his balance would be to fall downwards upon the deck, rather than up and over a three-foot high gunwale.

The most likely chain of events seems to be that William Scott was deliberately tossed over the side of the vessel, following a violent argument with either James Smith or William MacDonald. He was, remember, a strong and large man. Perhaps both men (who had grievances with the deceased man) planned to dispose of William Scott while his son slumbered drunkenly below deck? Conceivably, the inconsistent testimony offered by William MacDonald was in reality a deliberate (and risky) ploy suggested by his barrister, which had the desired effect of placing serious doubt in the jury's mind over Smith's guilt. After all, it seems that the Fort William police and Procurator-Fiscal were certain of Smith's guilt, probably based on his previous bad character and his reputation for hard drinking. However, it was a salutary lesson learned by the authorities, a murder charge in which they relied solely on the evidence of one witness was always likely to be too fragile a case for a Scottish jury.

William Scott's body was never recovered from its watery grave in Loch Linnhe, which reaches a depth of 150 metres at its deepest point. Therefore, no formal autopsy or search for evidence could take place. Without a body, a murder conviction is notoriously difficult to obtain. In fact, in Scotland's entire legal history, there have only been eight successful prosecutions for murder without a victim's body having first been located. None of these convictions took place during the era of the death penalty, with the first conviction not actually being achieved until 1975, and the following one not until 2010. In four of these eight cases, the murderer actually admitted their guilt.

Without a victim's body, an obvious motive, and only one witness, it seems that the prosecution's case was poorly prepared and presented. This may seem unforgivably sloppy on the part of the Crown; however, it is worth remembering, in 1874 the intelligence of the 'criminal classes' was generally believed to be so low that a conviction was often perceived to be a foregone conclusion. The reliability of the Crown's main witness was, in all likelihood, not considered prior to the trial.

It seems almost certain in this case, that the overstretched Fort William police did not anticipate their case being so easily derailed in the courtroom. In fact, partially as a result of this mistrial, the number of police constables stationed in Lochaber was substantially increased, under the terms of several *General Police Improvement Acts* which were enacted in Scotland between 1875 and 1890. When the police force had first been established in Lochaber in 1849, it had consisted of just three constables. Even by 1874, although the number of police officers had increased, its ranks were wholly inadequate to deal with the escalating number of crimes reported each year.

Perhaps the most intriguing question to arise from the trial
is the strange behaviour of William MacDonald during
the hearing at Inverary Courthouse. If he did falsify his
evidence, merely to help create an element of doubt in
James Smith's guilt, this seems to have been undertaken
only at great risk to himself. It must be remembered that,
when Constables Fraser and Macaskill first boarded the
Heather Bell at Corpach Harbour, William MacDonald's
clothes were bloodstained, while James Smith's were not.
MacDonald also freely admitted that he made little effort to
recover William Scott's body from the water, allowing it to
sink to its final resting place at the bottom of Loch Linnhe
(which he was openly criticised for by Lord Young during
the trial). This appears to be the act of a man with a great
deal to hide.

Yet, if William MacDonald was in fact the murderer of
William Scott, why was he not brought to trial, or (at the
very least) charged with perjury for his clearly misleading
evidence during James Smith's court hearing? The answers
to these questions are ones of legal interpretation under
Scottish law.

Firstly, despite the bloodstains on his clothing, the evidence
of James Scott indicating that MacDonald and his father
had argued, and MacDonald's misleading evidence in
court, he was not the subject of the trial. Once James Smith
had been found not guilty, all the same legal precedents
would then need to apply in any subsequent murder charge
and trial against William MacDonald. The case against
William MacDonald offered no confession, no witness
(since it had been established that James Smith and James

Scott were below deck), no real evidence of a crime (other than bloodstains, which in 1874 could not be proven to have come from the deceased man), and no victim's body. Therefore, if the first attempt at a murder conviction had been unsuccessful, the second attempt would also certainly have been doomed to failure.

Even William MacDonald's blatantly falsified evidence in court would go unpunished. In 1874, to a certain extent, the Scottish legal system still relied on series of principles set out in common law. A witness could not be indicted for perjury 'unless the alleged lie had a material effect on the outcome of the trial in which it was first spoken.' Because Lord Young had declared a mistrial in the case against James Smith, it could be said that the evidence given by William MacDonald did not bring about a wrongful conviction, since the case was abandoned before MacDonald's evidence was allowed to sway the jury or James Smith had been wrongfully imprisoned.

As a result, William MacDonald walked away a free man. He was never charged with either deliberately misleading a murder trial, or with the murder of William Scott (which technically remains unsolved to this day).

The law governing deliberate perjury was tightened and consolidated by the *False Oaths (Scotland) Act 1933*, which made some attempt to simplify the law in Scotland surrounding false oaths, statements, and declarations.

The limitations of the legal system and the difficulty in securing a conviction, conceivably allowed one – or possibly two – men to escape justice for the death of William Scott.

William MacDonald seems to have lived a blameless life after the trial of James Smith. At any rate, he was never in trouble with the police again. James Smith appears to have a turned over a new leaf after his narrow escape from justice. He renounced drink, married a young lady named Margaret, and opened a temperance hotel on the east coast of Scotland at which prayers and scripture were spoken three times daily for the spiritual benefit of patrons.

The body of William Scott remained unrecovered, and out of reach on the floor of Loch Linnhe. With it lies the answer to the question – who really killed William Scott?

THE GHOSTS OF LOCHABER

Scotland is often reputed to be the most haunted place in Europe, if not the world. If that is correct, then it may well also be true that the most haunted place in Scotland is almost certainly Lochaber. From the islands to the mountains, from the wilderness of Glen Coe to the bustle of Fort William, a ghostly reminder of the region's turbulent past is always just over your shoulder.

In 1871 a panic spread among the residents of Fort William and Spean Bridge when a farmer encountered a disturbing phenomenon, whilst feeding his cattle. The farmer, reported to be 'mild mannered, sober, and not susceptible to flights of fancy', entered his barn late one evening, only to experience a disquieting sensation. The farmer's vision was not a lone experience, however. In fact, the strange apparition was experienced by many in the district. Their descriptions were strikingly similar, enough to warrant a newspaper, church, and police enquiry.

Surprisingly, the ghost was not described as being white, glowing, or translucent; but rather black, solid and with intense fiery eyes. The events and descriptions of

the encounters were widely reported in the Scottish
newspapers:

*The peaceable and well-disposed inhabitants in the district of Fort
William have recently been much disturbed by the appearance
among them of a ghost, or something similar. The opinion,
however, was pretty general among those who actually saw the
incarnation - it was nothing else but the avowed enemy of mankind
in person; the devil himself come in spirit form. Of course, he was
black, with - if not eyes of fire - at least fiery eyes. His manner of
indicating his presence was through visions, and often startling
ones.*

*Here is an instance: A worthy old man, a farmer, who had ceased
to give credence to ghost stories, went one night to the barn for
the purpose of giving his limited stock of cattle their feed for the
night. There in the barn a large hogshead cask* (a 66-gallon
barrel) *where corn was kept, and in this hogshead the man heard
something moving. Being convinced that the noise was occasioned
by which ever rodents much molested his crop, the farmer proceeded
to the house, got a light and other contrivances, for trapping the
vermin, and went back to the barn. On the cask, however, his
consternation knew no bounds, when beheld peering viciously over
the barrel, the unmistakeable countenance of His Lord of Darkness.*

*According to witnesses, the cattle would not eat, and fasted that
night, but on looking into the cask next day, it was empty. Other
farmhands were called. The farmer's son was told to secure the
cattle in their respective stalls, which he did so, taking special care
to ensure the calf was safe and secure. But when leaving the byre
he was met by the same calf demanding admission. He was quite*

satisfied that he had previously put the same calf in its own stall, so, before giving it admittance second time, he went and consulted the other members of the family. The result was that the whole house came out carrying lights, and when they reached the byre, to their horror, they found the 'bogle' (an old Scots word for a phantom or goblin) *in the calf's place! Next morning a young man came to the farmhouse inquiring after his pet goat, which had been out all night and had gone missing, after he had seen a black apparition with fiery-red eyes during the night. The farmer and the young man went to the byre. But the ghost has not been seen since.*

There were several further sightings of this strange manifestation in the area surrounding Fort William, and the matter raised alarming concerns for a short period of time. Occurring more than a century after the abolition of the Scottish witchcraft purges, which mainly occurred during the seventeenth and early eighteenth centuries, these strange sightings do not appear to have been linked to witchcraft (despite the apparent sorcery). Instead, the occurrences appear to have been linked to either the devil and the growing movement in the occult, or to the restless spirit of a starving soldier, who was perhaps killed during the '45 rebellion.

A short journey southwards along the shores of Loch Linnhe will take the intrepid ghosthunter to Ballachulish, the community formed around the 'narrows' in the loch where the Ballachulish Ferry ran until the construction of the modern bridge in 1975. The area's association with the Massacre of Glencoe is just one of many reasons that the village is steeped in ghostly tradition. Deeper into the glen there have been abundant sightings of anguished clansmen and disembodied redcoat soldiers among the rocky mountainsides, graves and cairns; along with shadowy encounters at the Kingshouse Hotel (which features in the chapters *The Problem With Murder*). The wounds in Glencoe run deep, it seems. Yet, even to the west, by the picturesque confluence of Loch Linnhe and Loch Leven the land is soaked with blood.

On the south side of the loch, at this point, lie two buildings which seem to provide a direct link to that violent past, Ballachulish Hotel and Ballachulish House.

Ballachulish House was initially constructed in 1640 as a country estate. The house was occupied by Sir Robert Campbell of Glenlyon in 1692, after he had received the King's orders to put 'all the MacDonalds of Glencoe under seventy years of age to the sword'; leading to the notorious Glencoe massacre.

The original Ballachulish House was extensively damaged during the Jacobite rebellions of 1715 and 1745, and the current dwelling was rebuilt shortly afterwards.

The house is also associated with the murder of the king's factor, 'The Red Fox' Colin Campbell. In May 1752 Campbell led a detachment of British government soldiers into Ballachulish, to collect taxes from clan leaders and, no doubt, suppress any anti-Campbell sentiment. As his party headed into Lettermore Woods, Campbell was killed by a musket shot; at which point his assailant fled.

It is still possible to visit the scene of the murder; a signpost by the roadside will lead you inland and uphill to a cairn marking the spot with the inscription 'hanged on this spot for a crime of which he was not guilty'. The slaying of Colin Campbell is dealt with in more detail in my previous book *Blood Beneath Ben Nevis.*

In the aftermath of the Red Fox's murder the authorities launched a witch hunt in a desperate attempt to locate the culprit. In the frantic search for a scapegoat the soldiers arrested the unwitting James Stewart and imprisoned him in Inveraray Jail. Stewart was subsequently found guilty by a Campbell judge and jury and sentenced to death. On 8th November, James Stewart was taken to Ballachulish where he was hanged at a point close to where the southern end of the bridge now stands. A commemorative plaque marks the spot. His body was left to rot for several months, to be picked at by the birds, and as a means of disheartening any local Jacobite support. It is perhaps no wonder that Ballachulish House is reputed to be haunted.

Traditionally, there are two ghosts which can be found there – both in the grounds outside the house. Firstly, an apparition on horseback, possibly a soldier, approaches the house before dismounting, then mysteriously vanishes on the driveway, only to reappear and repeat the sequence. Secondly, there have been many sightings of a scruffily dressed man, short in stature, often seen close to the front gate, before he too disappears from sight.

Perhaps even more inexplicable is the story of Mrs Boulton, a lady who purchased the house in the late nineteenth century. Mrs Boulton arrived at the property for the first time, to be shown around by Lady Beresford, the previous owner, only to suddenly exclaim that she did not need to see the house, as she already knew it well from her dreams. Surprisingly, this revelation did not surprise Lady Beresford, who instantly recognised Mrs Boulton as 'the little lady who has haunted my house for years.' This story, it appears, was well known within the Boulton family and handed down through several generations, even appearing in the published obituary of Sir Harold Boulton in 1935.

Even more remarkably, according to a newspaper report at the time, this strange event was reputedly repeated during the 1960s:

A woman was driving through the countryside near Ballachulish when she noticed a "For Sale" notice outside of a large house. After knocking on the door she was shown around by an elderly woman. During the tour of the house the woman was struck by the knowledge that she already knew every room intimately. She was able to answer questions about the layout and geography of the house, without having ever been there before.

The elderly lady then explained to her prospective buyer, 'The house is on the market as it is haunted.'

The woman enquired further, 'I don't suppose you know who it is haunted by?'

The elderly lady exclaimed, 'The house is haunted by YOU, my dear!'

There seems to be similar versions of this slightly eerie tale recorded in several countries across Europe, and even in the United States, both in fiction and non-fiction. Coincidentally, most versions of this disconcerting tale seem to involve an elderly houseowner and a remote, rural setting.

Close to Ballachulish House sits the more recent Ballachulish Hotel. Dating from 1877, the gothic revival hotel sits on the site of a much older ferry inn. Used by travellers and drovers alike, this 'crossing of the water' is steeped in both history and hauntings.

Both guests and staff at the hotel have reported strange, ghostly apparitions and unexplained occurrences, some of which have even been photographed.

Two former employees of the hotel, Jim Morrison and Heather MacLeod, in addition to their own experiences, described several incidents of unexplained phenomena reported to them by guests and fellow staff members alike.

In 2010 Morrison recalled:

One day in room 112, I was helping Heather move a bed when we heard heavy footsteps coming along the corridor and stopping outside the door. But when I looked, nobody was there. Heather had experienced the same thing in the same room a few days before.

On another occasion, I was in room 204 when the window which normally stays open twice slammed shut when there was no wind or anything to cause it. Then, when I looked over to the bed, there was an imprint on it as if somebody had been sitting on it. There would also be strange feelings in certain rooms like you were being watched.

The former head receptionist at the hotel, Gwen MacAskill, also received reports of unexplained phenomena from guests over several years. Gwen explained:

There have been people who have mentioned things happening at the hotel. One guest, who stayed a couple of years ago, (2008) emailed us a picture he had taken in room 215 of what looks like a small boy standing beside the bed. One of our maintenance guys who has been here for 15 years has also spoken of seeing the boy in the picture. People have mentioned just feeling things in a couple of rooms.

In room 121, people say they have experienced seeing someone or feeling as though there is somebody standing in the room. Also in room 121, there was a driver staying a few years ago who was convinced he was being held on the bed by something and it wouldn't let him go. He also said how he had heard children's voices in the room. That room had been beside the children's nursery when the hotel was first built.

Other people have mentioned an old lady standing in corridors, while another time a member of staff was staying in a room while the hotel was closed when her partner heard footsteps coming down the corridor. When they looked, no-one was there, and the hotel was closed anyway.

A former night porter at the Ballachulish Hotel also reported hearing the sound of the hotel's piano being played. He decided to investigate; however, upon entering the hotel's lounge he found the room seemingly deserted and the piano apparently playing itself.

In 2017 a couple staying at the hotel reported a disturbed night's sleep, when they heard:

What sounded like someone inserting a key into our door. The noise was loud but a thought crossed my mind that it may be our neighbouring room. A little slow to react, I decide to sit up and as I do, I hear the noise of the door opening and then briskly closing. Without my glasses, I squint and can see from the bed that the door is closed but within seconds the bathroom door sways open with a gust and exposes more light into the room (we left the light on). Half awake, I took a few steps out of bed and turned the corner into the bathroom. No one was there and there's certainly no room to hide.

The phenomenon could not be explained.

During November of 2018 an American couple, Andy and Diane, suffered a similarly disturbing experience while staying at the hotel. Diane later described the night in detail:

Everything was quiet until the dead of night. It must have been around midnight when things began to happen. Andy was sleeping soundly beside me, so missed all of what followed. I didn't see any point in waking him, because although I felt deeply uneasy by what I could hear, I didn't feel that whatever it was intended to harm me. Nothing could be gained by both of us being awake anyway.

Just so you know, the door was very securely locked from the inside, including the door-chain. We generally travel with a lot of Andy's photography equipment which is very valuable and so are always security conscious. No one had, or could have, broken in without us hearing a lot of commotion.

To the left of my side of the bed stood a large double wardrobe. My wax jacket was hanging on the front of it. I'd hung it there because it was slightly damp from the November mist. In the dead of night something began scratching on my jacket. No more than two feet away from me, it sounded like long fingernails clawing up and down on the surface, quick, rapid movements, up and down, scratching. The sound was so close that I could have reached out and touched it. However, I didn't dare. I just wanted it to stop and go away. The scratching continued for several minutes as I lay there with my eyes wide open, afraid to move.

Then it stopped, and something walked across our creaky floorboards, passing by the end of our bed and headed towards the window. I could hear something being set down on the windowsill, followed by rustling in the left-hand corner of the room. I could vaguely see through the dark, and could see no one there. I would have been able to see a dense human form, and although the sounds were there, no form was present.

The footsteps across our floorboards continued back and forth for some time. At one point pacing almost desperately, as if to search for something outside the window. Whatever it was kept returning to that window overlooking the loch. Then it returned to my bedside, again scratching on my coat.

After two or three hours of laying absolutely still, Diane fell into a fitful sleep during which time she experienced an extraordinary dream in which she was transported into the bedroom opposite, then violently back into her own.

Instantaneously I was back on my bed, gasping for air. Andy was still laying peacefully asleep beside me. This time I did wake him up. I was visibly shaken, not having experienced anything remotely like that before. I told him about the night I'd just had and he really wasn't sure what to make of it. Knowing I'm not drawn to drama, he listened and heard me out.

Dawn approached. Nothing whatsoever had been disturbed in our room, despite the noise. I had a somewhat uneasy shower, then got dressed so we could make an early start. I must admit, I wanted to get out of that room.

Before heading downstairs for breakfast, my curiosity got the better of me. I had to know. I put my head around the door of the bedroom opposite ours, wanting to know if it looked the same as I'd seen it earlier. To my astonishment it did look just as I'd seen it. That was enough for me.

Without mentioning anything specific, over breakfast I asked the owner if any of his guests had experienced ghostly encounters during their stay. He looked at me, smiled and replied, 'Well funnily enough, when guests do mention it, it's only ever from one or two bedrooms in the old part of the hotel'.

With the brutal execution of James Stewart and the area's turbulent past it is perhaps no surprise that the Ballachulish House and Hotel have been linked to numerous ghostly and unexplained events. At least the tranquil waters of the loch must have provided visitors with a haven from these mysterious occurrences. Or so you might think...

In 'The Narrows' there is ancient rock known as Clach Phadruig or Peter's Rock, named after a Viking who stepped from the rock while trying to save his son from drowning. His tortured spirit is reputed to haunt the waters. Local tradition has it that the sheltered waters of Loch Leven were frequently used by the Vikings and, somewhere beneath the surface, there may be a Viking burial site. This may explain the phenomena of strange, white orb-like lights occasionally seen hovering above the water; and some of the mysterious deaths that have been recorded in the loch. In 1909 the son of a manager at the Kinlochleven aluminium works was drowned while fishing from a small boat on Loch Leven; something reputedly having disturbed him on an otherwise peaceful loch.

Just a few miles further south along the shores of Loch Linnhe, on a small islet in the loch, sits the fourteenth century Castle Stalker, home of the Stewarts of Appin. Here too, an orb of brilliant light was said to appear and hover over the castle just prior to the death of a Clan Stewart chieftain. Castle Stalker is inexorably linked to the region's violent history. During the 1745 uprising the castle was under the control of the Campbell clan, who allowed a garrison of around 60 Government troops to be billeted there. Although the Stewarts of Appin raised an

army of 300 loyal Jacobite followers, they were unable to
reclaim the castle. 2lb cannonballs fired from the Jacobites'
small-bore cannons merely bounced off the castle's walls.
Following the Battle of Culloden, Castle Stalker was utilised
by the government forces as a facility for the Clansmen
to surrender their arms. Those who fell foul of the *Act of
Proscription* were incarcerated in the 'Prisoners' Hole' at the
castle before being transported to Edinburgh for trial.

In 1861 a horse being ferried across the waters of Loch
Linnhe was disturbed by a frightening vision resulting in
yet another tragic death on the loch. The incident was
reported in several newspapers at the time:

*On Sunday, 22nd September, 1861 Mr George Macquay, an
English gentleman, twenty-six years of age, residing with his
mother, Mrs Creed, at Culchenna, near Fort William, met his death
under the following circumstances. He had been paying a visit that
day at Ballachulish House, the residence of Mr and Mrs Unwin,
and between four and five in the afternoon left Ballachulish to
return to Culchenna, which is on the north side of the Ballachulish
Ferry. The ferryboat being in readiness at the pier, with two
boatmen at the oars, Mr Macquay stepped in, accompanied by his
groom in charge of his riding-horse, and the boat was rowed off,
and in ordinary circumstances would have reached the other side
in less than five minutes. It seems that the horse became restive after
a mysterious white vision appeared from the Loch, and in panic,
turning round in the boat, the horse came in contact with Mr
Macquay, who happened to be standing on the gunwale near the
stern, and, losing his balance, he fell overboard into the water. At
this time the boat was not more than sixty yards from the shore. Mr
Macquay, though a remarkably powerful and active young man,*

was no swimmer; but he contrived, by great muscular exertion, to keep his head above water for some seconds each time he rose to the surface, and he was seen to go down and reappear three times.

The boatman, despite being much disturbed and afraid by the strange happening, was, in the space of about two minutes able to reach him an oar, by which he kept himself afloat till the other men in the boat got to his assistance, and dragged him in. Having been brought ashore, and carried to Mrs Christie's inn, close by, every attention was bestowed on him. To the joy of every one present, he was able to converse a little, and appeared to be in fair way of recovery; but after the lapse of an hour he felt oppressive on the chest, with great difficulty of breathing, and a suppressed cough; and within another hour he breathed his last. The medical opinion is that the unfortunate young gentleman died, not from drowning, but, by the violent muscular exertion on his heart caused by the ghostly vision, and by his attempts to keep afloat and regain the boat. Mr Macquay was a gentleman of singularly handsome appearance and polished manners, and was a great favourite in the district. His untimely end is deeply regretted, and much sympathy felt for his widowed mother, the deceased, having been the last survivor of a large family.

Perhaps the explanation for the mysterious disturbances surrounding Ballachulish lie, not under the bloodstained soil after all, but beneath the inky surface of the loch that borders the village. It seems that the troubled past of Ballachulish may run as deep as the waters that surround it. Perhaps in Ballachulish there is indeed blood across the water?

MURDER OR MISTAKE?
THE OBAN KILLING

Monday 19th February 1934 had been much like any other day for Alexander Clark and James McAllister. The two men operated a coal delivery business and were busy plying their trade around the wintry streets of Oban. The weather had been dry but cold, and demand for fuel kept the two men busy.

In the late afternoon, Clark and McAllister stopped their open-back lorry outside the premises of the local dentist, Mr McDougall, in Argyll Square, adjacent to the Royal Hotel. Alexander Clark stood smoking and leaning against the side of the lorry, while McAllister carried a sack of coal inside the premises. As Clark waited, he noticed an older man staggering along the street towards him, in the direction of Albany Street. Even in the gathering darkness, Clark recognised the man instantly as a rival coalman, who operated another coal round in the town. The man's name was Hugh Martin. He was in his forties, and lived with his brother Donald in Drimvargie Terrace, just a few minutes' walk away. As Hugh Martin approached the coal lorry, he appeared dishevelled and the worse for drink.

His reputation as a drunk and a troublemaker preceded him but, on this occasion, Hugh Martin did not seem particularly troublesome.

The two men chatted briefly. Alexander Clark told Hugh Martin that he should probably go home, 'as you seem a little the worse for drink'.

Martin replied, 'Don't worry, I'm a game kid!'

The two men continued a friendly chat, until they were interrupted by another man walking purposefully towards them. He was younger than Hugh Martin, no more than twenty-three or twenty-four. As he approached in the gloom, it was now just after six o'clock and the sun had set. Clark recognised the young man as Thomas Ledwidge, an attendant at Boni's Billiards Room in the square.

Ledwidge was walking in the middle of the road. He walked up to Clark's coal truck and, interrupting the two men's conversation, he addressed Hugh Martin aggressively, 'What did you say to my missus?'

Hugh Martin leaned back nonchalantly against the truck and said 'Nothing, but if you think I did, I can scrap you any minute.'

The men argued and Hugh Martin swore aggressively, although he made no attempt to make the altercation a physical one. Suddenly, without warning, Thomas Ledwidge struck Martin across the face with his clenched right fist. The blow was hard and direct, and Martin crumpled to the ground. Seeing the older man on the road, Thomas Ledwidge turned his back on Martin and walked off in the direction of the fountain. Alexander Clark and James McAllister, who had now finished the coal delivery, helped Hugh Martin to his feet. The two coalmen advised him to go home and jumped into the cab of their lorry to drive away. However, as they drove off, Clark looked back from the cab of the lorry and noticed that Hugh Martin had instead followed Thomas Ledwidge across Argyll Square. As he approached Ledwidge, Martin waved his fists and gesticulated wildly. Ledwidge pushed Martin away with his left hand, but this did nothing to persuade the older man to desist. Ledwidge again struck Martin with a direct blow on the right side of his face, and he fell instantly to the ground. This time he lay motionless. Thomas Ledwidge looked at him for a moment before turning around and walking off in the direction of George Street.

Later that evening, Hugh Martin's brother, Donald, was finishing his dinner at 7 Drimvargie Terrace when he heard a sharp knock on the door. He got up to see what the commotion was, only to be met by two police constables who were carrying his elder brother. Hugh Martin was unconscious and could not be woken. Between the three men, they carried the unconscious man upstairs and put him to bed. After the police explained to Donald Martin that his brother appeared to have been involved in a fight and had been found lying in Argyll Square, the younger sibling agreed to sit with him until his condition improved, also promising to summon the doctor if his brother took a turn for the worse.

Sadly, Hugh Martin did not recover and died shortly after midnight without ever regaining consciousness.

Oban police launched an immediate murder investigation and made a hasty appeal for witnesses to come forward. It was not long before the name of Thomas Ledwidge was given to the authorities, and he was duly arrested. He was then formally charged at an initial hearing:

Thomas Joseph Ledwidge, of Oban, formerly of Motherwell in Lanarkshire, you are charged that you did, on February 19th 1934, assault Hugh Martin of 7 Drimvargie Terrace, Oban, by striking him on the head and face with your fists, and knocking him down, whereby he received injuries from which he died on February 20th, and you did thus murder him.

Ledwidge protested his innocence to the crime of murder; however, bail was refused, and he was led away to be held on remand at Barlinnie jail in Glasgow, while preparations for his trial were made.

Cases of this seriousness had been few and far between in Argyll for many years. So few, in fact, that the tradition of the Circuit Court sitting at Inveraray Courthouse had not occurred for twenty-six years. The pomp and ceremony surrounding the arrival of the judge, counsels, and associated dignitaries, was to be specially reinstated for the trial of Thomas Ledwidge.

Finally, after almost six weeks on remand, Ledwidge was to be tried at the High Court in Inveraray on Tuesday 27th March 1934. The trial was expected to last two days.

Following a pre-trial gala dinner and reception, a military guard of honour comprising fifty men of the 8th Argyll and Sutherland Highlanders was provided for Lord Wark. They formed in front of his hotel and escorted him, together with a throng of local officials, on the brief journey to the courthouse. Pipers played, and the judge's arrival at the courthouse was greeted with a fanfare of trumpets, in the Scottish Circuit Court tradition. The compact courthouse was packed; every available seat was occupied. Those who were unable to find a seat stood against the walls and filled the window ledges. Those who could not gain entry lined Church Square outside.

The era of the death penalty always ensured an especially charged atmosphere inside Scottish courtrooms. The tension was obvious to all those inside, as Lord Wark was approached at the outset of the proceedings by Thomas Ledwidge's defence advocate, Mr Thomas David King

Murray, KC, who was regarded as one of the leading counsels of his time. He informed Lord Wark that his client wished to enter a special plea of self-defence. This was duly noted by Lord Wark who reminded the defence team that it was the task of the jury to decide whether this was the case.

With the preliminaries completed, the prosecution, led by Mr John Cameron, Advocate-Depute and assisted by Mr DM Campbell, called their first witness, the murdered man's brother Donald Martin.

Mr Martin, you are the deceased man's brother. Can you describe him for the court.

Yes, he was forty-eight years of age, and being honest, he had a weakness for drink. But he was quite harmless.

In cross-examination Mr King Murray asked, *And when your brother was drunk, was he provocative and quarrelsome.*

No, sir. He was not.

Mr King Murray continued, determined to paint a picture

of the deceased man, *Did he take to drinking methylated spirits?*

The craving was there.

I have here a list of twenty-six convictions against your brother, dating from 1926 to 1933, for molesting the police, being drunk and incapable, assault, and committing breaches of the peace. Are these all true?

Yes, replied Donald Martin, *that list is correct.*

Next, Alexander Clark, the coalman, described the events of that night, detailing the blows dealt by Ledwidge to Hugh Martin, *Ledwidge let go a blow at Martin with his right fist. Martin dropped and James McAllister and I lifted him up. Martin was in a fighting sort of mood. Then he struck him on the face and Martin fell straight back. It was more of a jab than a blow.*

Mr Joseph Boni, the owner of the Argyll Square billiard room and shop below, where Thomas Ledwidge worked, was next to testify. He was able to shed some light on the events leading up to Hugh Martin's death:

On February 19th I heard a scuffle coming from the shop downstairs. Anne Ledwidge, the wife of the defendant, was employed by me there. She called out 'Tom, Tom!' Thomas Ledwidge was at the far end of the billiard room and did not hear her call. I went downstair to see what was wrong, and I saw her and two other customers attempting to put Mr Martin out of the shop. He was very drunk and shouting and bawling. He needed to be put out. I saw him attack Mrs Ledwidge in an indecent way. He then put his arm around Mrs Ledwidge's waist and asked her 'Will you marry me?'. We put him out and told him not to come back.

Afterwards, Mrs Ledwidge told her husband what had happened, saying 'Hugh Martin was getting fresh'.

Next to be called by the prosecution was Dr Andrew Currie from Oban, who was asked to read details of his post-mortem report to the court:

On examining the body of the deceased, I found a contused lacerated horizontal wound, about half an inch in length, on the victim's scalp. There were no other signs of external violence. Death was due to intracranial haemorrhage, caused by external violence by some blunt agent at the back of the head. In my opinion his injuries are consistent with a fall.

Mr King Murray, for the defence, interrupted with a question, *Have you determined if the deceased had been drinking, and if so, had he consumed methylated spirits?*

My examination showed that the man had been sodden with drink. Although I do not know what he may have consumed on the day of his death.

Thank you, Doctor, Mr King Murray continued, *it appears that the deceased man had drunk methylated spirits in some quantity previously. As well as being morally degrading, would you agree that the continued consumption of this spirit would have a negative effect on a person's body.*

Yes, there is certainly medical evidence that a large amount of drink or methylated spirit consumed by a chronic alcoholic has an effect on the arteries, whereby the blood vessels of the brain tend to more easily rupture than normal.

Thank you, Doctor.

On hearing both the medical evidence and the testimony of Mr Boni the case took a surprising twist. John Cameron, the Advocate-Depute, approached the bench and requested a reduction in the charge sought by the Crown from one of murder to the less serious charge of culpable homicide:

Your Lordship, it is obvious from the evidence given here that the charge originally levelled should not be proceeded with. We propose to reduce the charge to one of culpable homicide.

I think you have exercised a wise discretion, Mr Cameron, replied Lord Wark.

The charge of culpable homicide is unique to Scottish law, although it is similar to that of manslaughter under English law. It can be described as an offence where the accused has caused loss of life through wrongful conduct, or wicked recklessness, but where there was no intention to kill. The reduction in the charge sought by the Crown was not necessarily good news for Thomas Ledwidge, however. Culpable homicide also carried a lengthy prison sentence. In addition, it might now mean that the jury was more likely to find him guilty of the slightly lesser charge, since the onerous duty of sending a man to the gallows had been lifted from their shoulders.

Mr King Murray now began the case for the defence by calling his only witness, the accused man himself, Thomas Ledwidge:

Mr Ledwidge, please, in your own words, explain the events of the 19th February for the court.

When I heard of the incident with my wife, I intended to go to the police station and lay a charge against Martin. I was on my way to the railway station to get an evening paper first when I met Martin in Argyll Square talking to Alexander Clark, the coalman. I did not expect to find him there. I said to him, 'Keep your filthy hands to yourself next time.' Martin then asked me, 'Is it a fight you want?' and he challenged me to a fight. I then hit him on the chin, but saying that, it was more of a push than a blow. I then walked off, but he followed me and tapped me on the shoulder. I could not get rid of him. He nagged me, used filthy language and waved his hands in an aggressive manner. Then he dropped his hands to his side. I was afraid that he was going to pull out a beer bottle which I could see in his trouser pocket. So, I struck him again, but not hard. I had no intention of hurting him badly. I walked away after that.

Mr King Murray then summed up the case for the defence, telling the jury that his client had been incarcerated in prison for almost six weeks on the most serious charge, when the evidence had always been that the offence simply did not justify a charge of murder.

Lord Wark's final summation carefully briefed the jury on what the law expected from them. In order to convict the accused of culpable homicide, the judge explained, the jury must be satisfied that Thomas Ledwidge had assaulted Hugh Martin, contrary to the law, and that the assault had resulted in Martin's death. On the other hand, if the members of the jury thought that the 'smart blow' delivered by the defendant was merely a means of ridding himself of Martin's unwelcome attentions, without any intention of inflicting harm, then they must find him not guilty. He added that the jury must interpret the type of blows inflicted on the deceased man, which had been variously described during the trial as 'a smart blow', 'a jab', and 'a push'.

With that, the jury retired to consider their verdict.

An anxious Thomas Ledwidge, and all those in the crowded courtroom, did not have to wait long to hear the outcome of the jury's deliberations. The jury returned after only eight minutes and delivered a unanimous verdict of not guilty. This was followed by cheering and applause from the public gallery, which caused Lord Wark to rebuke those present by saying, *'This is a court of justice! It is not a theatre!'* Perhaps, in the heat of the moment, he had forgotten the irony in his remark, following the pure pageantry which had preceded the trial.

Half an hour later, Thomas Ledwidge, together with his wife Anne in her grey fur trimmed coat and black beret, emerged from Inveraray Courthouse to be met by a jostling and cheering crowd in Church Square. They were quickly whisked away by motor car to Oban to rebuild their lives after the harrowing trial which, in the era of the death penalty, may have resulted in an appointment with the hangman's noose. The prosecution's decision to ask for a verdict of culpable homicide might have conceivably swung the trial in the Crown's favour. Had, for example, the deceased man been a more sympathetic character, and the defendant a less sympathetic one, the verdict may have been a very different one.

Wishing to put the events of 1934 behind them, the couple appear to have moved away from Oban following the trial, firstly back to Motherwell, before eventually returning to their birthplace in Yorkshire.

The jury in their deliberations ultimately chose to place their faith in Thomas Ledwidge's version of events, and on the expert medical evidence given at the trial, believing that his actions were purely in self-defence and that he did leave the billiard hall to buy a newspaper from the kiosk at the railway station and not to seek a premeditated and angry confrontation with Hugh Martin. The fragile state of the deceased man's health, caused by his sustained consumption of alcohol and methylated spirits, together with his previous criminal record and drink-fuelled rages, clearly contributed to his own demise.

The jury's confidence in Thomas Ledwidge seems to have been well placed. He had been a man of previous good character and led a blameless life following his release before eventually passing away in 2001 at the age of ninety.

Following the trial, Lord Wark thanked the people of Argyll, stating that he sincerely hoped it would be at least another twenty-five years before a serious case was tried again in Inveraray. In fact, the case of Thomas Ledwidge v The Crown was to be the last High Court trial to be held in Inveraray. During the 1950s the circuit court town for Argyll was moved to Oban, leaving the courthouse empty.

Inveraray courtroom and jailhouse now serve as a museum, telling the story of the many notorious prisoners and trials held there.

ACKNOWLEDGEMENTS AND BIBLIOGRAPHY

Acknowledgments:

This book has been made possible thanks to the continuing support, granting of permission to use material, and for your valuable knowledge and resources: Kevin and Jayne Ramage, Highland Bookshop Fort William, Aberfeldy Watermill Bookshop, Vanessa Martin and everyone at the West Highland Museum, Georgie Burns, Alexa Reid, Ellen McBride, Lesley Christian, Angus MacDonald, Diane Nicholson, Fort William Library, Inverness Highland Archives, National Library of Scotland, Find my Past, Family Search, Scottish Index Archives, Inveraray Jail Museum, Lochaber Archive Centre, Lochaber Local History Society, Ancestry.com, British Newspaper Archive, International Newspaper Archive, Electric Scotland Archive, National Museum of Scotland, Martyn Downer, National Archives Kew, London Underground, Scottish Law Archives, The Independent Order of Rechabites, Dalmally Parish Church, National Maritime Museum, Lloyds of London, Bank of England, and to anyone that I have inadvertently missed out. Your help was gratefully received.

Bibliography:

The Wreck of The Annie Jane, by Allan F Murray, *Bathymetrical Survey of Freshwater Lochs,* Royal Collection Jacobite Letters, *Blood Beneath Ben Nevis,* by the author, *English Society 1660-1832,* by Jonathan Clark, *1715: The Great Jacobite Rebellion* by Professor Daniel Szechi, *Waverley,* by Sir Walter Scott, *Culloden,* by Murray Pittock, The Diary of James Boswell, *Scottish Legal Tradition* by Lord Cooper, *Principles of Criminal Law in Scotland,* by Archibald Alison, *The '45,* by Stuart Duff, *Bonnie Prince Charlie,* by Sir Fitzroy MacLean, *The Lighthouse* by Keith McClosky, *Lochaber and the Road to the Isles* by Christopher Uncles, *Prisons and Punishment in Scotland* by Joy Cameron, *Hundred Years in the Highlands* by Osgood Hanbury MacKenzie, *Scottish Historical Documents* by Gordon Donaldson, *Jacobites* by Jacqueline Riding, *Gaelic Dictionary* by A Armstrong, *A Very Civil People* by John Lorne Campbell, *History of the Hebrides,* by WC MacKenzie. Neil MacEachen's Journal 1746, *Scottish Field, Oban Times, Aberdeen Evening Express, Alloa Advertiser, Glasgow Herald, The Scotsman, Edinburgh Evening Express, Dundee Courier, The Press and Journal, Perthshire Advertiser, Dundee Evening Telegraph, Forres News, Glasgow Evening Post, Evening Citizen, Inverness Courier, Inverness Journal, Daily Telegraph, Daily Express, Daily Mail, Evening Standard,*